TOGETHER WE ARE
Stronger

WE ARE ALL DIFFERENT, YET THE SAME

A division of International School of Story
Savannah, Georgia

www.marigoldpressbooks.org

Copyright ©2021 Emra Smith

Library of Congress Cataloging-in-Publication Data
Smith, Emra 1959
Together We Are Stronger

Library of Congress Control Number: 2021921290
ISBN: 978-1-942923-53-4

Cover Design by Aimee Burchard Pearson

Fonts licensed for use.

Bible versions used are noted within the text,
and belong to the copyright holders thereof.

TOGETHER WE ARE *Stronger*

EMRA SMITH

WE ARE ALL DIFFERENT, YET THE SAME

Dedication

*For my people who are different than me,
yet have showed me that we are all the same.*

My first friends who loved me, a stranger in their city, Patrina Lingard and Clarissa Lighthouse Johnson.

My friend from a country afar who became family, Joanna Rulewska Wilson.

My daughter and friend who has a mental challenge, Candice Wagener.

My mentors who vary in age: Juanita Kretschmar, my prayer warrior; my daughter, Lianro WagenerSmith.

The men who became my brothers, Andre van Heerden and Gregg Talbert.

My girlfriends who have laughed and cried hard with me over the years, Sandra Pieterse, Deanna Pitchford, Karen Pearson, Sharilyn Smith, Vinetta Willis, Tina Allton, Anna McCoy and Shaillee Chopra. Even though we're all so different, our hearts are the same.

My husband, Robert. We couldn't be more different from one another and yet so the same. You have taught me the essence of what respect is and unwittingly challenged me to live it out loud. What a gift! Thank you. I love you.

To each of you, thank you. You have enriched and expanded my life.

Contents

Introduction 10

Preface
    Understanding Respect 14
    Stereotypes, Bias, Prejudice, Judgment 15
    Key to Success to the Simple Fix 18
    The Six Aspects of Diversity 20

PART ONE

Because of Race & Ethnicity 24
    Dawn Baker: Single, Satisfied, Sharing 26
    Susan Call: Living with your Lions 34

PART TWO

Because of Disability 42
    Shaillee Juneja: Stepping Into, Blossoming, Soaring 44
    Kiri-Maree Moore: Solutions Disrupting Pathways 50

PART THREE

Because of Generations 60
    Victoria D'Natale: Bullied But Not Beaten 64
    Helen Campbell: Forgiving the Unthinkable 70

PART FOUR

Because of Gender *78*
  Jenny Lynn Anderson: From Complex Quietude to
                              Outspoken Survivor *80*
  Sarah Williams: Storms and Peace *88*

PART FIVE

Because of Socio-Economic Standing *96*
  Janet Swanson: One Voice with Global Impact *98*
  Georgette Jackson: Upheld and Holding Up *106*

PART SIX

Because of Personality and Emotion *118*
  Tina Allton: The Power of One Increasing the
                              Power of Many *120*
  Dawn Knighton-Adkins: From Prostitute to Pastor *128*

CONCLUSION

Speaking Up *138*

With Thanks *141*
About the Author *142*

*I have a dream that one day every valley shall be exalted,
every hill and mountain shall be made low,
the rough places will be made straight and the
glory of the Lord shall be revealed
and all flesh shall see it together.*

Martin Luther King, Jr.

Introduction

We Are ALL Different, Yet the Same

Inherently, we are all entirely different from one another. We live in the same city, yet are from different parts of the world, have different skin colors, speak varied languages, and eat different foods. There are people in our workplaces that use a wheelchair or hearing aid, that cannot read or write. Our community is filled with millennials, boomers, veterans, men, women, gay, and straight. Friends, family, and strangers range in personality styles with varied levels of disposable income and capacity for emotion. Add to this the many experiences that impact our stories and voilà—we differ majestically from one another! YET we are essentially ALL the same!

We are all human. We share the basic survival needs to have food, water, air, sleep, shelter and safety, but whether consciously or not, there are a few core aspects we all seek after. In his Control or Choice Theory, Dr. William Glasser teaches about four need groups: the need for love, belonging, and connection; for power, significance and competence; for freedom and autonomy; and for fun and learning.

There are other theories about the needs we have. Each theory varies slightly. According to author Anthony Robbins, the six core human needs are certainty, variety, significance, growth, contribution, and love and connection. The first four needs are defined as needs of the personality and the last two as needs of the spirit.

The Bible teaches that ALL of us are created equal, and that when Jesus came He unified us: "For He Himself is our peace, who has made the two groups one and has destroyed the barrier, dividing the wall of hostility" Ephesians 2:14 (NIV).

"But in our time something new has been added. What Moses and the prophets witnessed to all those years has happened. The God-setting-things-right that we read about has become Jesus-setting-things-right for us. And not only for us, but for everyone who believes in Him. For there is no difference between us and them in this. Since we've compiled this long and sorry record as sinners (both us and them) and proved that we are utterly incapable of living the glorious lives God wills for us, God did it for us. Out of sheer generosity He put us in right standing with Himself. A pure gift. He got us out of the mess we're in and restored us to where He always wanted us to be. And He did it by means of Jesus Christ," Romans 3:23-24 (MSG).

"For all have sinned and fall short of the glory of God, being justified as a gift by His grace through the redemption which is in Christ Jesus," Romans 3:23-24 (NASB).

Regardless of which verse or theory resonates with you, it's clear we ALL have core similarities.

Enbra

SO, I have a dream . . . A prayer for you. . .

*Just as I have taken action in
teaching these concepts and writing this book,*

I PRAY THAT YOU

*Take action with me . . .
Choose to overcome your bias and prejudices,
To live with respect and kindness,
That you would choose to love one another . . .
even though we're different,
because we're really all the same.*

#TogetherWeAreStronger

Never lose sight of the fact that the most important yardstick of your success will be how you treat people—your family, friends, and coworkers, and even strangers you meet along the way.

Barbara Bush

Preface

Understanding Respect

What is respect? *Dictionary.com* says it is: "Esteem for, or a sense of the worth or excellence of a person, a personal quality or ability. Proper acceptance or courtesy. To show regard or consideration for."

Is it easy to understand "respect" by those definitions? Respect is how you treat people. Or should I say, how you should treat people. Why is it so difficult to consistently show respect toward others? Why not see the good in each person, versus what annoys and irritates? Why can we not accept one another's differences without putting the other person down, insisting on change and arguing? Why do you feel anyone is less deserving of their needs being met than you are?

I think it is because we are innately selfish. Our survival instinct demands it of us. Our first communication skills protect us. A baby cries when hungry, if he or she didn't, the baby would starve to death. Quickly, babies learn to cry when uncomfortable. What would happen if they didn't? As they grow, we teach children to consider the needs of the family. Think of those terrible two's and trying three's, then teenagers—fighting for independence and to have their own voice. For them, it's all about "me."

During the journey of physical growth, inherent DNA leads each of us to acquire our attitudes, skills, personality styles, strengths and weaknesses. We also develop bias, stereotypes, prejudice and often, unconscious judgment of other people and situations. It is so easy and comforting to put people in boxes that fit our point of view.

Stereotypes, Bias, Prejudice, Judgment

Stereotypes are oversimplified images or statements applied to a whole group of people, without regard for each individual. It happens when we see a person of a specific culture and immediately assume they're an illegal immigrant, or that they have a certain religion. It happens when we think that people with disabilities aren't fit to work in all workplaces. Perhaps we stereotype when we think people with mental illness are dangerous. Unconscious stereotypes that stay unchecked can lead to a negative bias.

Bias is a predisposition to see events, people or items in a positive or negative way. Bias is an attitude or belief. We see things not necessarily as they are, but we see them as we are. We see through the lens of our upbringing, culture, country of origin, family, education, communities, disposition, or personality type. With this immense variation for each of us, who is right and who is wrong? We all have bias toward many things and people. The skill lies in becoming aware of them and guarding against the negative attitudes they instill deep within us. Unchecked bias breeds prejudice.

Prejudice is an unfavorable opinion formed without knowledge, thought or reason. Unchecked, prejudice hurts, harms and diminishes respect for others. It separates communities, families and societies. This impacts productivity in the workplace, healing in churches and unity in communities, which all diminish strength and positive growth in a nation.

Bias and prejudice leads us to judge one another, often subconsciously. We form opinions, which lead to actions that impact our behavior, often creating a breakdown in relationships, even leading to possible harm. Wayne Dyer made this powerful statement, "Judging others does not define who they are, it defines who you are." Wow!

The Bible spells it out so adequately: **Do not judge!**

> *Judge not, that you be not judged.*
> *For with what judgment you judge, you will be judged;*
> *and with the measure you use, it will be measured back to you.*
> *And why do you look at the speck in your brother's eye,*
> *but do not consider the plank in your own eye?*
> *Or how can you say to your brother,*
> *'Let me remove the speck from your eye' and look,*
> *a plank is in your own eye? Hypocrite!*
> *First remove the plank from your own eye,*
> *and then you will see clearly to remove*
> *the speck from your brother's eye.*
>
> Matthew 7:1-5 (NKJV)

It's so easy to see how communities, cities and countries around the world are crumbling due to a few critical aspects. Namely, a lack of respect for one another, clinging to bias, prejudice, judgment, and stereotyping one another cause much of the breakdown of society today.

Yet it's so simple to fix! We can accept that we are all the same, yet we all have differences. Respect the differences. Don't judge. Once again, the Ancient Book spells it out clearly, with ease and power:

*For this is the message that you heard
from the beginning: love each other.*
1 John 3:11 (CEB)

*Be always humble, gentle, and patient.
Show your love by being tolerant with one another.
Do your best to preserve the unity,
which the Spirit gives by means
of the peace that binds you together.*
Ephesians 4:2-3 (GNT)

*Prejudice is a burden that confuses the past threatens
the future and renders the present inaccessible.*

Maya Angelou

Key to Success for the Simple Fix
Understanding Diversity – Our Differences

Diversity: the art of thinking independently together.
Malcolm Forbes

There are many ways we are different from one another. We are going to look briefly at six aspects of our differences in this book. You can easily research each of these aspects for more depth, learning and current statistics. Following each aspect of diversity, there are two stories of women and what happened when God entered their lives. You will see how diverse the stories are, how different each woman is, and yet how similar, and how God empowered her life and purpose. Each story does not necessarily reflect a specific aspect of diversity, yet it shows each experience is challenging in one way or another.

It does not matter who we are, where we come from, if we are disabled or not, what age or gender we are, how much money we make, what our personality is, or what experiences we have had—each of our stories matter.

Each of our strengths, gifts and skills, so unique to each of us—makes the family, church, community, workplace, and country bigger and better. With each diverse aspect, society can run optimally.

Your Story Matters.
You Matter.
Every day, in every way. Always.

Together We Are Stronger

*Two are better than one; because they
have a good reward for their hard work.*
Ecclesiastes 4:9 (CEB)

Our body does not just have one part. It has many parts.
1 Corinthians 12:14 (CEV)

*My children, our love should not be just words and talk;
it must be true love, which shows itself in action.*
1 John 3:18 (GNT)

Alone we can do so little; together we can do so much.

Helen Keller

The Six Aspects of Diversity

Chester Barnard, American author of pioneering work management theory and organizational studies, said, "Once you have understanding, you can get cooperation and connection." I pray that you will allow yourself to see any bias, prejudice or judgment of others you may have. Ask God to show you what might be hidden in your heart. Acknowledge it and let Him remove it. Don't judge yourself. At times, these beliefs, emotions, and attitudes come from past experiences or observations of pain and injustice. Have the courage to get help if your problem is deeply rooted. You merely must make a decision to choose change.

Will you choose to see within each of these following differences how they actually strengthen our communities and our world? Will you choose to see with me, that even though we are all the same, our differences make us beautiful and interesting?

Say with me today:

> *Together we are stronger despite differences in*
> *ethnicity and race,*
> *disability,*
> *generation,*
> *gender,*
> *socio-economic status,*
> *personality style or emotion.*
>
> #TogetherWeAreStronger

Cease the busy.
Change the hurried cup of coffee for a soothing cup of tea.
To accentuate the letting go of bias,
prejudice, and judgment of others,
Change the flavor of your tea, or how you normally drink it.
Perhaps cold tea will become hot tea.
Your regular black tea will have a little milk in it today.
Add a little honey or spice.
Experiment, be creative, have fun with it!
Perhaps you change your cup.
Pick a fancy one, a brightly colored one,
a mug, a crystal glass.
Smile. Embrace the change.
Get comfy. Sink into your favorite chair.
Sip and be soul-stirred as never before.
Be empowered.
Receive HOPE through these stories.

Grow your faith. Gain courage and strength.
Receive peace as you enlarge your world
By embracing others unconditionally.

YOUR Story Matters.
Each story matters. The big stories. The little stories.
Each one, every day.
Your entire life matters.
You matter.

PART ONE

Together We Are Stronger

Because of Ethnicity and Race

Together We Are Stronger
Because of Ethnicity and Race

The word ethnicity presents various aspects—language, culture, traditions, religion. Perhaps you're thinking of each of these aspects in terms of what yours are or perhaps that of a neighbor. I have become quite enamored by the Southern culture I now live in. The deep Southern drawl is so different from my South African British sound. I've become accustomed to sweet tea over ice instead of hot tea. I've adjusted to living in the buckle of the Bible-belt, where any given secular meeting begins with an opening prayer. I've adopted the tradition of the Thanksgiving holiday and my favorites, celebrating the 4th of July and Juneteenth, when enslaved African Americans were notified of their freedom.

These are just a few of the joys I've found in this small section of the diverse American nation. Imagine how diverse the many ethnic aspects are here! There are ten affinity groups recognized: Black, White, Hispanic, Multiracial, Asian, Native American, Alaska Native, Native Hawaiians, Other Pacific Islanders, and the MESA group, which is made of Asian Indians, Middle-Easterners, and North Africans. And this is just the United States of America. What about all the countries of the world? We mix and mingle, trade and do business with each other, support each other, learn and grow from one another. Even if all we learn is what *not* to do, we still learn!

It is incredible how vast and multi-cultured this world is, yet how interdependent we are on one another. We are dependent on each other even if we are a self-sustaining nation. If one country trashes their water or air it impacts us all. Over population has a ripple effect no one escapes. We need each other. We are all connected, yet we find our sense of being in our own tribe. We seek 'our same' among the diversity we live in.

Henro Tajfel says, "Social identity is a person's sense of who they are based on their group membership. Groups give us a sense of social identity; a sense of belonging to a social world. In order to increase our self-image we enhance the status of the group to which we belong. We are the best! We discriminate, we hold prejudice, which results in racism—and in extreme forms results in genocide. We create "them" and "us," the in-group and the out-group."

A few examples of in-groups and out-groups are: in Northern Ireland, the Catholics and Protestants; in Rwanda, the Hutus and Tutsis; in Yulgoslavia, the Bosnians and Serbs; in Germany, the Jews and the Nazis; in political America, the Democrats and Republicans; in football, the Clemson Tigers and Georgia Bulldogs; in gender, the males and females; in social classes, the independently wealthy and the working class.

What is your in-group? What is your out-group?

Will you choose to not judge those in your out-groups?

Can you respect the differences of all groups without prejudice, bias and discrimination?

It takes two flints to make a fire.
Louisa May Alcott

Dawn is a woman with poise, beauty and energy. She emanates an energetic charge as she enters a room. It would seem there's not a person in Savannah who doesn't know her. I met her personally the first time she invited me to her morning TV show. I couldn't miss the strength of her sense of purpose, which innately grounds her. I treasure the moments we can connect in her crazy-busy life!

Dawn Baker

Single, Satisfied, Sharing

I'm a Georgia girl, a privileged girl. Not because we had wealth, or status—we didn't—but because we had love. My mom and dad were young parents and I was an only child. They divorced before I was three. My mom found work as a teacher about forty minutes away from where we lived, so my grandparents, aunts, uncles—everyone—cared for me.

I had an old-fashioned upbringing. I played with the neighborhood kids and when the sun went down, I knew I had to go home. Everyone was connected and we took care of each other. Growing up I learned to work with people and to help people. If anyone fell on hard times, neighbors always stepped in to help.

Like our outlook on life, the food we ate was wholesome. My granddaddy had a farm and grew almost everything we ate. As children, we helped in the fields. It was rare for us to buy food from a grocery store. There were always fresh vegetables, pecans, and chickens. Whenever we had more than we needed we traded what we had with each other.

Nights at home were quiet. Sometimes we would stay up until midnight when the National Anthem came on TV. When the song was finished and the screen displayed fuzzy snow we knew it was time for bed.

Life was simple and good. As their first grandchild, my grandparents spoiled me. On the other hand, my mom was the family sheriff—all law and order! Now I tease her about the way she was, but it was no laughing matter back then. I didn't realize how blessed I was until I grew up and realized the lessons my family taught me prepared me for the real world.

I had so much love and support I didn't realize my dad was absent. When I was twelve years old, I was with my grandmother at the grocery store and a stranger walked up to me and hugged me. I had no idea who the man was or what was going on. Grandma explained, "That's your daddy, baby."

He only lived five miles from me but never came to see me before meeting in the store that day. He visited me five times the next year. When I was thirteen we moved to Savannah and he stopped showing up.

I heard from him again when I was twenty-six years old. He called when his dad passed away. He started telling me about his other children. He said, "You have eight-year-old twin sisters. They don't believe you're their sister because you never visit them."

I was angry because he is the one who abandoned me, not the other way around. In my pain, I ended the conversation and have not heard from him since. His friends tell me he brags about me but he has made no effort to get to know me.

When we moved to Savannah, I was a freshman at Savannah High. Some of the students bullied me because I was the new kid and my mom and I lived in a house as opposed to public housing. I spoke in complete sentences and not in the cultural dialect. The other students didn't accept me. The girls were mean to me. They bumped into me on purpose and threw paper at me in class. I was very isolated. There was no way I would tell Mom about it because I was afraid she'd say something to the administration and it would make the bullying worse. Thankfully, the football coach saw what was happening and looked out for me. By sophomore year, the bully-girls backed off. I believe it was because they finally became used to me.

After graduation, I went to Howard University and majored in Broadcast Journalism. I missed my mother so much I would cry, yet college turned into an amazing experience. There were people from all parts of the world and I was able to meet them and learn from their experiences.

My first job after graduation was in Wilmington, North Carolina. I felt excited as my career was falling into place, but I was not prepared for the racism I would encounter. I had quite a difficult time finding an apartment, though most had vacancies. When I finally found a place, it was on the sixth floor of a building where the elevator was broken. My landlord warned everyone that I was moving in. I lived alone on that floor for six months until some college students moved in.

My first day at work as a reporter, just days out of college, I thought I would shadow a reporter to learn the ropes, but that wasn't the case at all. Instead, I went on-air and reported a news story that very first day. I was assigned a story about a fire in which three children were killed. It was the second story in our newscast. We were minutes from the newscast airing, and I was so stressed my head was pounding. I called my mother and told her I couldn't believe I was going on-air.

My mother has always been my greatest supporter and toughest critic. She said, "Weren't you hired to be a reporter?" She was right. I gathered my strength and spent the next year working as a reporter and fill-in talk show host at WECT-TC. The News Director thought Dawn was a wimpy name so he used my initials, D.G. Baker, on the show.

My precious grandmother became very ill that year. My mom moved her into her home. I knew I needed to move back home and help take care of my grandmother. My mom did not want me to leave my job to come home, but it was time for me to make decisions about my life. I worked hard to find a job and moved back after securing a reporting position in Savannah. It was the first time I ever ignored my mom's advice, and it was the best move I have ever made.

WTOC-TV was looking for a reporter with three years of experience. I only had one year. I literally wore down the manager, Doug Weathers. I called him constantly and sent him new resume tapes each week. I was relentless. He hired me and I've been at WTOC since 1989. For me, each day is not about the big story we feature, but it is about helping viewers when they feel they have nowhere else to turn. It is an honor to help the people of my community every day.

It saddened me as I began to see many children in my community making mistakes and destroying their lives. They never learned lessons they needed to cope with real life and were not prepared for life's setbacks. As I look back at my imperfect history, I realized how blessed I still was. I am who I am and have what it takes to survive because of my family. I realized I could be the family some of the kids around me didn't have.

I did not have the joy of having children myself, as my husband and I divorced after three years of marriage. The girls in my community became the daughters I never had. I felt inspired to show them who they could be regardless of circumstances.

I wrote a book, *Dawn's Daughter: Everything a Woman Needs to Know*, and started the *Dawn's Daughter Leadership Academy* for 9th and 10th grade girls. Each year, I award *The Dawning of a Miracle Scholarship*, which enables a young woman who has a chronic life-threatening illness, or who has achieved in spite of adversity, to start college. While I dreamed of helping young women, I never realized what a blessing they would be to me. Sometimes it breaks my heart to watch the many struggles the young people endure; they inspire and encourage me as they overcome life's many complexities.

I have also been blessed to go on life-changing medical mission trips to Ghana, Guatemala, and Nigeria with the *Goodness & Mercy Foundation*. The people in the countries we visit face such dire circumstances, but their attitudes and spirits are amazing. I've learned so much from them. As well, each trip gives me a greater appreciation of the great nation America truly is.

I will never forget how the children jumped up and down as our buses rolled into their village in Ghana. There were more than a hundred people lined up at the medical mission site waiting for hours before the clinic was scheduled to open. They considered Tylenol a miracle drug there. Regardless of their poverty, the families rallied around the children. They made sure their kids took education seriously. By the time they were in second grade, most of the children spoke more than three languages!

I wish Americans valued education the way those villagers do. Too many of us have become lazy, believing the government owes us and should supply all of our needs. Many don't realize assistance programs are designed as stepping-stones during dire times and are not a way of life. I could have easily fallen into that line of thinking, following the easier way as many people around me did. I am thankful God placed me in the loving arms of my family—my mother, grandparents, aunt, and uncle—who empowered me to be more than the status quo.

My family never allowed me to buy into what others expected of me because of who they thought I was. I came from what they called a "broken home" in the 70's. I was black and we were poor. My mom made all my clothes. She even sewed in labels that said, *Designed by Lula Baker*. I learned that education was the most important thing in life. With it, I could write my own ticket and live on my terms and I did.

I'm thankful for my knowledge, career and life experiences. God has allowed me to use each aspect of my past, both positive and negative, to help others. I always try to live by these words by the Dalai Lama XIV:

Every day, think as you wake up, today I am fortunate to be alive, I have a precious human life, I am not going to waste it. I am going to use all my energies to develop myself, to expand my heart out to others; to achieve enlightenment for the benefit of all beings. I am going to have kind thoughts towards others, I am not going to get angry or think badly about others. I am going to benefit others as much as I can.

To connect with Dawn or to invite her to speak, send an email to: dbaker@wtoc.com. Find Dawn's book, **Dawn's Daughter: Everything A Woman Needs To Know,** *at www.dawnbakeronline.com*

*A dream you dream alone is only a dream.
A dream you dream together is reality.*

Yoko Ono

She briefly stood up at the She Speaks Conference and spoke with excitement about her book release, giving us a glimpse of her story. The first chance I had, I went to her, we sat down, and she shared more about her book. I was stunned. Susan Call is a gentle, soft-spoken woman who knows and trusts God; her confidence in Him breathes hope and peace.

Susan Call

Living with Your Lions

I was under the illusion marriage was easy. Perhaps that thought came from watching my mom and dad, who are still married today. I also thought the tradition of going to church equaled Christianity. Without much thought, I happily married. Little did I know I had just entered into a difficult relationship that would challenge me to the core. Through it all, I discovered Christianity is more than going to church; it is a real relationship with Jesus.

My husband was an alcoholic, abusive and irrational. Our relationship put my heart and soul into grave despair, but I kept going. I was working and we had two little children to care for.

As I commuted to and from work, I'd listen to stories of Jesus on the radio. I heard stories of incredible trials and hope. I hungered for hope. I started believing God would show up and make everything right. Instead, everything went wrong and I started seeing reality; my situation was harmful. My husband confessed he was in a relationship with another woman and that she was going to move in with us for a week. He told me I better stay or else! With horror, I discovered the other woman was our babysitter! I previously felt she was like a sister to me, but now I felt deep betrayal. My husband threatened to end my life if I left. I felt trapped and couldn't even protest.

Charles Stanley's daily radio programs impacted my life profoundly during that dreadful, dark time. As if God ordained, he came on tour to a city near me and I was determined to attend. At the meeting, Charles Stanley told the story of his encounter with a wise older lady who showed him a picture of Daniel in the lion's den.

The woman asked him, "What do you see?"

He responded by telling her everything he knew about Daniel's story.

After he finished, she looked at him and said, "You're missing the point. Daniel was standing amidst lions, but he was focused on God."

The illustration struck home in me. As I walked through each day of my twisted marriage experience, I kept remembering Daniel in the lion's den. I needed to keep focusing on Jesus and He would keep me safe. I owned that truth and kept trusting in God. I believed for and experienced His protection as I stayed focused on Him.

One night my daughter woke up screaming from a dream. "Daddy sent you to heaven," she cried.

Knowing that fear had gripped my child's life put me over the edge. Hearing her voice of truth cleared up my denial of the situation and adrenalin kicked in my drive to protect my children. I did not want my children to live in fear, or to be exposed to the depth of loss, and resulting anger that would come from brutally losing their mother.

I carefully planned for six months before we fled that house. I did my research and learned that 75 percent of women die from domestic abuse *after* they leave because of increased anger and retaliation from abusers. I couldn't risk that, so I didn't plan my escape alone. I sought help from a private investigator. Plans fell into place and the Lord opened doors and provided a way out.

My private investigator told my children to look for purple cows as we drove out of town and journeyed on. The kids did just that; they didn't once look back. They only looked ahead with anticipation.

How poignant for me. What was I focused on? The abuse? My fear? The horror we had endured? Fear of being unsure of what was to come? Look forward, Susan, look forward!

Upon arrival, I discovered the place we moved to was near Charles Stanley's church. God provided both a physical home and a spiritual home! He is truly in the details and always adds the exclamation point! God kept showing up in various ways to remind me He was watching out for me even though I lived in a state of heightened awareness every day.

Despite being safe, at one point I continued to really struggle. I knew all God had done for me, yet I had a pile of growing prayer requests. I felt stuck.

Nothing was changing, everything felt trapped in limbo, just sitting there, even my spiritual growth.

"God, why am I no longer growing spiritually?" I asked.

He answered clearly. "Because you are holding tightly onto things in your curled up finger-fists. Your hands are full; there's no room for more."

I realized I needed to let go of everything, even the blessings. I had to be fresh and available for what was next, focused on the future. I had to let go of the way I viewed God in order to allow Him to work in a new way in me. Once I let go, God made me ready for the next step.

I received a call concerning the custody hearings of my children and was advised not to go. The wiser choice would be for my children and me to receive new identities. This decision drove me to my knees in prayer the entire night.

God gave me a new name and a new identity—Danielle Matthew. Danielle after Daniel, whose story inspired and challenged my life, and Matthew, as a new beginning after the first book of the New Testament, which shares the newness of life that comes from Jesus to the entire world. Peace filled my soul as I grew in my identity as God's daughter.

Then, I clearly heard His voice. "Go back. Attend the court hearing, and one day I will call you to share your story for Me." In strength, I stood up knowing that no matter what trial I faced, I was His, and had a new identity in Christ.

Going back felt like returning to the lions' den. It was so suffocating and close. It felt as if the lions were breathing in my face, but I still stood tall. The court ordered me to move back to the area we left, as the judge ruled in favor of my children's father.

I didn't understand why the custody hearing turned out that way. I was jaded, but God reminded me that He was faithful and I was to focus on Him. I wrapped our lives up in God, and constantly ran to Him during each encounter with my ex-husband's irrational behavior and moments of deep ugliness. I had to focus on God and not the lions.

I was heartbroken, a single mom, and could see my children needed me more than ever before. My entire life was in discord. I felt the world was a challenging, harsh place, yet I found hope in God as He navigated me through the difficulties.

God was with me in my brokenness. My heart questioned, "How can these pieces fit together?" My possibilities were so limited. I desperately needed better finances and more time with my children. I prayed fervently, pouring my heart out to God.

A short time later, I met someone who had a friend who needed the skills I had to offer. I could shift my hours so that I no longer needed childcare, which freed up both finances and time. I learned not to limit God!

One day after school, my son came home saying, "Mommy, I fell today." A few days later he said, "Mommy, I fell twice today." That evening, he walked across our tiny apartment and fell. "Mommy, that's how I fell at school," he explained.

Deeply perplexed, I took him to the doctor. He tested positive for muscle deterioration. The doctor told us the disease was not curable, and therapy would merely slow down the process. My son started falling so much his legs became quite bruised.

We went to church, and my son stepped out in faith when they asked for prayer requests. He asked for prayer to stop falling. Miraculously, he never fell again! Mysteriously, the latest lab test of his bloodwork was lost. God showed up mightily in our lives and healed him.

God further blessed us with a blended family which grew us to eight after I remarried. Several years later, I felt terrible physically and knew I had to go to the hospital as I had a congenital heart problem. At the hospital, they found my artery had a 90 to 95 percent blockage and I would not have even made it to the next morning had I not come in.

After surgery, I nearly died from complications and was in a critical condition. An attending nurse implied I obviously still had a purpose and God was watching out for me. I believe He has a purpose for each of us while we have breath and He uses both the beautiful and the broken.

In the fall of 2011, I went to an inspirational conference. I made a note on my notepad while listening to one of the speakers: "I need to write." It was if God said, "Now I have your attention and it's time."

I wrote during the busy time of November and December, yet I completed the manuscript, which was not humanly possible without divine help. I remembered when God told me I would share my story for Him and now I was pursuing God's call.

I entered my manuscript into a contest. In August of the following year, I found out I won and they published my book in the self-publishing arena. After about six weeks, I received a call from a traditional publisher who offered me a contract to publish my book, *A Search for Purple Cows*.

God flung every door wide open. I never had to write a book proposal, or research publishers; it all divinely happened! My book was released in October of 2013, and since that time I have heard from people everywhere who read my story. The furthest away I've heard from was India and Mexico.

I have learned not to limit God according to my understanding or experiences, and to keep my focus on Him. I no longer listen to or stare at the lions around me. I listen to God affirm me, and thank Him for His ingenious plan that lies before me. In the face of lions, my praise became rich and free.

Susan Call is the author of A Search for Purple Cows *and speaks for Jesus wherever she can. If you would like to have her speak to your group, contact her at www.susancall.com.*

Because whatever you think about the most will grow.
This applies to both the positive and negative ends of the spectrum.
Dr. Caroline Leaf

PART TWO

Together We Are Stronger

Because of Disability

Together We Are Stronger
Because of Disability

Google states the word "disability" means a physical or mental condition that limits a person's movements, senses or activities. Disability is about acknowledging what limits a person has, and recognizing that the person is not the disability. In short, we must put people first, see their value, individuality, and capabilities.

With the Americans with Disabilities Act of 1990, the US Equal Employment Opportunity Commission provides a list of conditions they conclude as disabilities:

> *deafness, blindness, an intellectual disability, partially or completely missing limbs, mobility impairments that require the use of a wheelchair, autism, cancer, cerebral palsy, diabetes, epilepsy, HIV/AIDS, multiple sclerosis, muscular dystrophy, major depressive disorder, bipolar disorder, post-traumatic stress disorder, obsessive compulsive disorder, and schizophrenia.*

As I read about disability online, I learned that many injuries and medical problems cause disability. Some injuries may resolve over time and are considered temporary disabilities. An acquired disability is the result of impairments that occur suddenly or chronically during the lifespan, as opposed to being born with the impairment.

Living differently because of any of these disabilities is part of life. Any one of us can be disabled in the blink of an eye. There is so much we learn from one another during the difficult moments of life. Let us support one another when needed, remembering that though we may be different, we are of the same essence. We have many similar needs, even when they aren't verbalized. Patience, courtesy and respect for people are integral cornerstones of a healthy community. We must be inclusive of those that are differently-abled than us. And honestly, don't we all do life differently from one another? We just need to learn to see each other as "able" versus "disabled," as we truly are each "differently-abled" in our own way.

Will you choose to see people first and not their disability?

I don't need easy. I just need possible.
Bethany Hamilton

Shaillee signed up for my coaching class, Write Your Story. The call of her heart beckoned that it was her time to share what stirred inside. Her multi-faceted story, poetry and powerful voice of hope, needed to be shared with the world. Within a few short months, we became soul sisters, combining our gifts to share hope globally. What a joy, honor and gift Shaillee is to me, and to the work we do together.

Shaillee Juneja

Stepping Into, Blossoming, Soaring

Born in India into a lineage of restless, ambitious, visionaries, life's purpose was bigger than ourselves. I struggled to fit into the box.

My grandfather migrated to India from Pakistan and was an active participant in the political and social movement of the early 1900's. He was a part of the freedom struggle for India, a social revolution that promoted education, women's rights and access to education for women. He was an author, wrote in seven languages, had a printing press, started the first college for women and lived a long prosperous life until the age of 94.

His restless ambition was passed on to my father, who left home at age 14 to join the navy, becoming their youngest diver. He was an extraordinary man who never saw things for what they are, but for what they could be. Once married, he and my mom had two daughters, and chose to see having girls as a gift. In our culture, a man was seen as burdened and not blessed if he had no sons, yet my father's heart was full. To celebrate daughters, he would visit new families and give them candy when girls were born.

Dad encouraged me to be who I was, not be or do what culture or others dictated. He taught me to not be what I *should*, but to be what I *could*. My culture was one of "should's," but my father was one of "could's." He wasn't an understood man. He lived by that same restless ambition of his father.

He was a man with purpose who was born not to just come and live, but to be truly alive!

He traveled often, which exposed him to different cultures and facets of life. He settled our family in India. Those were tough years as he tried to fit into the structured norms of society. I saw his struggle and how he felt stifled, longing to be free. I watched my mother carry the burden of watching my father struggle to fit in, yet wishing for freedom. It seemed we could never just be at peace, living life with ease.

As the oldest child in the family, I inherited that same restless ambition. I learned to stifle the restlessness, not wanting to be a burden to my mom. I tried to be content living with the "should's." I *should* be a good daughter. I *should* come to the USA and earn well. I *should* get married, and I *should* have children, even if it meant eight years of infertility. I should pay for my mom and sister's education. I did all the "should's."

As I reached my 40's, I arrived at the junction of seeing who I truly was. My journey of liberation and finding my own path began. It was a journey of unveiling my potential and unabashedly owning it. There is hope when you fully embrace who you are. You are limitless when you can truly live versus merely living. My journey began by seeing the truth—all of it.

My first memory of depression goes back to when I was three years old. I had the same mood swings my father had. Some days, he didn't want to get out of bed; other days he had high energy, high ideas, was very happy, or very angry. We didn't know it was depression. We thought he just had mood swings.

In my 20's, I experienced depression but didn't know it. I had that sinking feeling that caused me to not want to get out of bed. It felt low and dark. Fear of failure and fear of not living up to expectations gripped me. I felt it in my body in cycles.

I started becoming exasperated in my late 20's going through infertility treatments. I had to take up to six shots a day and ten pills. Those drugs messed up my hormonal cycle and increased my risk of depression and anxiety. I did not understand that I was pre-disposed to those conditions. I went through eight years of infertility treatments, and five miscarriages, before our two boys were born. After each birth, I experienced postpartum depression which lasted six to seven months. Depression became a cycle, a way of life for me. Because I grew up with it, my only response was to be strong, tuck it away, and go through life silently. I survived through having grit.

During these times, thoughts of suicide would visit me. By divine intervention, I never had the courage to act on those feelings. I just wanted it all to end. My hope was that I would not exist much longer.

When I entered my 30's, I realized my mood swings were not a choice, yet still couldn't talk about it. I had the impression that mental illness was being crazy, being weak. I didn't have help to encourage me to embrace my emotions, or that I could get better. For two decades of my life, I walked that dark path. When I spoke to my close friends and family, I'd hear them say, "You don't have depression. Be positive! Be strong! You have a great family and career. Be positive, strong and pray about it."

I finally learned that depression is a condition, not a choice. I had, however, not learned that self-care needs to be a priority. In my early 40's I found a way to stay ahead of the depressive cycles. I could over-compensate. My achievements made me stronger externally and nullified my imperfection. I excelled to heights both in my career and socially with a great family.

Within a few years this all led to what appeared to be a cardiac arrest on a flight for work. At a follow-up visit with the doctor, I learned it was a panic attack. I was convinced I was not going to take meds and that in a couple of days I'd be back on my feet again. This didn't work and I started unraveling. This experience, that I now see as a divine intervention, compelled me to talk with the doctor about depression and anxiety. He placed me on the high functioning, bipolar, spectrum! I was in shock. It was the worst-case scenario I could imagine for myself, as my judgment against mental health diagnoses was so strong. I knew I couldn't simply put this label behind me. I went for a few more assessments, hoping someone would deny the diagnosis. Oh, how I buried my head in the sand.

I discovered I had a deep-rooted shame and fear against mental illness. "Mentally unstable people are psycho, and a burden to families they're born into," I thought. I was petrified someone would find out about me. I didn't want to be the imperfect person who burdens her family. I spent four months in denial. As my shame peaked, I isolated myself.

A couple of friends shared some profound words with me. They said, "This does not define you. It is just one aspect of you, not who you are." I agreed to go to counseling, which was instrumental for me. I educated myself about bi-polar and anxiety, and the physical reasons behind it. Finally, months into the year, I decided to get on the meds, taking three months to find the right dose. The side effects of the medications can be harsh, and until you find the right meds, they can make you feel worse.

I also found a support structure and started group counseling with the National Alliance of Mental Illness (NAMI). Finally, finding the dosage that worked for me, I started to feel better, yet unsure if I could return back to my high-flying career. I wondered if I could still perform or not. I have discovered that I can!

I have learned the key to a balanced life is self-discipline and self-care. Prioritizing exercise, healthy eating, meditation, and self-awareness is critical. Finding and practicing good technique is key.

I have come through this storm stronger, and have started to see the gifts it has brought me. Shifting my lifestyle and bringing me closer to my faith, I rebuilt a successful career, and even expanded it. I have shed layers that have been weighing me down my whole life. First I had to admit to every thing by saying it out loud, and embracing it fully. Now, I have become whole again. I still have highs and lows, days when I don't feel 100 percent balanced. I don't see those days as a weakness, but as something that is uniquely me. I've learned to capitalize on my highs as I become creative. In my lows, I practice self-care.

A gift through it all was finding a new purpose. I am to be a voice of hope about mental illness. The voices of others facilitated my steps to healing and purpose. If I can help someone off the ledge of suicidal thoughts, going through all of this is worth it for me.

If you would like to connect with Shaillee and to purchase her book, **Dear Brown Girl**, *contact her at Shailleejchopra@gmail.com.*

Act and God will act.
Joan of Arc

She sat quietly, listening, relaxed, yet aloof, at SXSW in Austin, Texas. She is from New Zealand and Australia, and I from South Africa and America. She was clearly not comfortable being in a crowd. Her dress-sense, her manner, compelled me to seek time with her alone. I am so glad I did. Little did we know how much we would laugh and share our passion to impact humanity together. Kiri-Maree is an exceptional woman. Strong, driven, kind, brilliant. A woman of impact!

Kiri-Maree Moore

Solutions Disrupting Pathways

I was given up for adoption when my 16 year-old birth mother had me, so I have never met my biological parents. The memories I have during the early time of my life are minimal. As a foster child, I moved in and out of five or six homes before the age of five, then lived with one family for nearly ten years before being kicked out. During those young years, I experienced a lot of abuse, physically, sexually, and emotionally. Finally, at age 14, I found a home with my best friend at school, and her family became mine. I tried to be perfect as I entered her perfect world, but I didn't feel perfect inside. I was the only one who knew the stories of my past.

For two years, my life looked awesome, and in many ways it was. Yet my internal battle was only beginning. I was triggered into an eating disorder, and spiraling downhill when my boyfriend looked at me and said, "You're fat."

My family was trying to save me from suicide, so I ended up in treatment in hospital where I was told I was dying of anorexia. I was at a crossroad. I could choose to let go of life or believe there was more to my world than what I had experienced. Physically, I wanted to give up. Yet somehow, from deep within, I chose to say, "You know what, I made it to this point in my life, there must be more. There has to be more. I was born to do bigger things than merely survive. If I was meant to be dead, with all the things I had already faced in my life I should have been dead already. There must be a purpose for my life. God must have a reason for me. I better find out what this truly is and make it happen."

My life was fixed overnight, but I was at the start of a huge journey. I was ready to fight for my life, to find out what it is I was called to do, and to use my life to help others.

As a teen, I started working with street kids, prostitutes, the hurt, and the needy. I looked beyond my lack, saw the needs around me, and began to make a difference in the lives of others who had lost the hope that they could ever achieve anything. The more I began to focus on others, the more I could see there was more than just me to keep fighting for.

Going through the aftereffects of anorexia, I dealt with bulimia. The external battle versus the internal battle was real. I tried to fit in and it was hard. My thinking was different than those around me. I had to work hard to get good marks in school, due to my struggle with dyslexia. I was always the different one, and I hated being different. As the years went by, I knew I had a big destiny, and I was not going to give up until I found it.

Clarity started unfolding after I went on a team trip to Hong Kong when I was 17. We spent time in the corruption of the Walled City, run by the Triads. The alleys were so low you could see the fluid drip of urine everywhere, and rats the size of cats. It was a place where the police didn't even go. My experience there opened my eyes to a world where help was needed.

The first day I walked in that place, I saw a 70 year-old woman and a seven year old girl sitting in a drain on the side of the road. They were both prostitutes waiting for their next act to survive their environment. Inside the Walled City, human beings living in cardboard boxes. When I walked back outside the wall, I saw fancy hotels on the other side.

Wealthy people walked by just one wall away, oblivious to the needs just a few feet away from them.

My placement was in a house for women and children who were, or had been severely addicted to drugs. At the house, they became clean and began new lives. It was a place of safety, and provided the possibility for a future. The opportunity to be there, to grow in my own thinking and to use the little I had in my hand, changed me.

I saw hurting people, and my heart broke as I realized that everything I went through didn't matter anymore. I had an opportunity. I had a choice to make something of my life, to see needs and to be a voice. From that moment on I never looked back. I did not realize that my experience there was changing me dramatically.

Around that time, I had an unexpected pregnancy. Whoops! In my family, that was not a good thing, especially after all they had done for me. Eventually, I found the courage to tell family, and they told me I needed to marry quickly. They found a man and we married within the month. Overnight, it was a marriage filled with violence. It felt as though all the abuse from the past had caught up with me yet again. It was a scary year where I wondered what the outcome would be for my newborn and me.

One night, my husband had his hand on my neck. I could barely breathe. With everything in me, I quietly called out, "God if You are real, now is a freakin' good time to show up." For a split second the man let go, releasing his hand. It gave me the opportunity I needed to escape, lock myself in a room, and call for help. After my initial rescue, I was told to return. I had to go back. He lived in one room and I lived in the other. For four months I was back in the cycle of fear and abuse.

On that horrible night where my husband choked me, I became pregnant again. I knew that for the safety of my child in the crib and for the one in my womb, I had to plan an escape. One day when he was out, I packed my car. It was one of the scariest non-negotiable things I have ever had to do. We escaped before he returned. I promised myself that if I ever had kids, my kids would never go through what I went through as a young girl.

Now more than ever, I had to find the strength to break the patterns from the past. I had an out. I had to focus and not look inward. I was determined to do whatever it took. I began to dig deep to learn why some people thrive and others do not.

I began to research and work out how to survive. My biggest hope now was for my kids to have a better future than my past had been.

I owned my truth when I messed up. I knew mistakes did not need to determine my destination if I began to make different decisions. I began to work on my next best self. I put myself through school and began therapy. Through therapy, I looked for help to ensure I would not bring my past into my future. I leaned on an amazing faith. I was bent on helping the world and not accepting the negative the world wanted to give me.

I was a single mom for at about five years. I focused on creating a world for my children to learn, grow, love, and add positive to the world. It was not the white picket fence life, but I strived to give them the best opportunities to thrive. I worked hard, left New Zealand, went to Australia and studied music, theological subjects and leadership. I didn't exactly know how my life would unfold professionally, but I knew I wanted to use my skills to change lives.

Over time, I saw that even though one can put on great programs to help change people's lives, once I walked out of their lives, most of them fell back into their old ways as the mess underneath the hope remained. I didn't want to just be a band-aid any longer. I wanted to help remove the root cause of problems and help achieve long term change.

I wanted to give access to sustainable resources and tools. My direction of work became very creative. I used music, productions, and hosting amazing events. I was a youth speaker for many years. I used what I had in my hand to make a difference, particularly in young people's lives to give them hope for a future.

My new story started at age 22, and continues to this day. I remarried and we've been together over 20 years now, raising a family of six children. I am a GIGI now too! Several of my children have special needs, yet we don't let this stop us in any way. Some of my children who are on the autistic spectrum have taught me a lot about being a better communicator.

One can use what others may perceive as a weakness to be a bonus strength. My son, who had many difficulties growing up, is one of my heroes. I have watched him work through challenges and grow into an amazing young man full of wisdom, spunk, and full of humor. I learned that my differences are now my strengths. I am a better, more effective leader when I stand in the strength of my differences.

Life took a radical turn for me ten years ago. I slipped. My husband mopped the floor, but didn't realize I always dry the floor after mopping. I didn't know the floor was wet, so I slipped and was severely injured. Up until this point in my life, I had been in the fitness industry for a number of years. I was super healthy, fit and lean. I moved with confidence.

After my fall, I was in a wheelchair for a year and a half. It was another crossroad. The injury messed up my brain. At the one-year mark, I was told, "Sorry, sweetheart, you have it so bad in your body, you will never be able to get out of this wheelchair." As I sat on the bed, I knew had two options. I could either sit there, not even able to get up and go the bathroom, or choose to get up and walk again, despite my pain being off the charts.

Once again, I faced the call to a bigger purpose than my current life. The consequences of my decision wouldn't only affect me, but would affect many others as well. I didn't come this far in my life to end up with Complex Regional Pain Syndrome and Fibromyalgia determining my outcome.

I knew I couldn't tell my kids to do whatever they need to do and fight if I did not lead by example. I wanted to know I was leaving a legacy full of possibility. If I was truly to be an amazing leader, how could I do it from my bed? I knew I had to make a difference through leadership, and I began fighting for my power once again. And fight I did! I even had to fight the medical community many times. Even today, they don't see how I can live without depression considering my condition.

I researched what I was going through at the time and found there was a one percent chance I could physically overcome. I chose to be the one percent. I used strategies to ensure I would reach victory. Each day started with a grateful moment. I stated three things I was grateful for from the last 24 hours, and three things I was grateful for in my next 24 hours.

Once again, I choose to have an outward-focus. Hearing them say, "Sorry, you will never get out the wheelchair," was good for me because it compelled me to find a way to make this seeming impossibility become possible. I asked myself, "What is my next step? My next level? What things do I have to do to get to my next step?"

First, I had to get out of the wheelchair. Then I had to move from using two walking sticks to one stick. Then I moved to a cane, a fitness walking stick, and finally to trying hard to walk without any aid. I kept focusing on what was working, not on what wasn't working. It is was a long-term mission, and I succeeded.

My next adventure came when my husband Taki and I started a business. Our company is now called Million Dollar Coach. We help coaches and consultants attract, convert, deliver, and scale client businesses. I remember the days of baked beans, two-minute noodles, and borrowing money off a friend to buy groceries. Now we travel the world training and speaking as nomad CEO's of our multi-million dollar company. Our family has been nomadic for two years. We are living and learning on the road, traveling the world, and teaching our children to explore life.

I am also the Founder and CEO of my own company, Decision Velocity Global. I help leaders to increase the diversity percentage of their top decision tables, and to make the right decisions quickly. I am also the Founder of VOICEadvocacy Foundation and The Leaders Movement.com where I advocate and give a voice to the frontline of humanity. I get to bring about change that inspires sustainable, scalable growth. I don't have it all perfect, I just continue to remain focused on the bigger vision.

My strength comes from my faith in a God who obviously never gave up on me. I live with purpose knowing that there is a bigger vision beyond who I am. Anything is possible. My life mantra is, "No Excuses. No limitations. No Buts!"

An outcome will unfold as you grow in your capacity. I never knew that what I do now would look like this. I get to work with the leaders across the globe and travel to all the corners of the earth changing lives. I've learned I'm good at disrupting the norm, creating innovation and seeing the dream alive even when you can't see how it is possible. That's why giving up is never an option. Our only option is to keep going and see results.

For more about Kiri-Maree go to www.TheLeadersmovement.com.

The power of one, if fearless and focused, is formidable, but the power of many working together is better.
Gloria Macapagal Arroy

PART THREE

Together We Are Stronger

Because of Generations

Together We Are Stronger
Because of Generations

Generations are fascinating! We see a glimpse of history in each person's story. A story gives us the opportunity to see where one is in the life-cycle—young adult, middle-aged, senior. We see how discoveries, events, progressions and experiences impact each generation collectively.

We have the Traditionalists, our Veterans, generally born between 1900-1945. They experienced WWII, the Korean War, the Great Depression, and saw the rise of corporations. They experienced hard times growing up, followed by times of prosperity for some. Typically, they adhered to rules, conformed, sacrificed, were disciplined and patriotic, respected authority, and were hard-working and loyal, to name a few core values.

Then there are the Boomers, the "Me" generation, born between 1946-1964. They experienced the Civil Rights Movement, the Vietnam War, the sexual revolution, the Cold War with Russia, and space travel. This generation has the highest divorce rate in history, and have the highest number of second marriages in history. These post-war babies grew up to be radicals in the 70's and yuppies in the 90's. They pursued the American dream and were seen as materialistic, greedy and ambitious. A few positive core values include the fight for equal rights and opportunities, an "anything is possible" mindset, optimism, personal growth, transformational power, strong work ethic, and willingness to take on responsibility.

These generations are followed by Gen X, The Doers, born between 1965-1980. They experienced Watergate, the energy crisis, dual income families, single parents, latchkey kids, Y2K, activism, corporate downsizing, the end of the Cold War, and most moms working. Generally, they favor balance, diversity, entrepreneurship, fun, high education, skepticism, global thinking, and working to live. Though some have a strong sense of entitlement, most are still willing to take on responsibility.

Then we have the Gen Y or Millennials, born between 1981-1996. It was a time of digital media, a child-focused world, with school shootings, terrorist attacks, AIDS, and 9/11. Many of this generation grew up as children of divorced parents. They were more sheltered than any previous generation, and the first generation of children with schedules. Some of their core values include achievement, confidence, diversity, fun, and personal attention.

Following on, we have the Gen Z/Centennials born between 1997-2015. This generation believes in openness, "you do you," resilience and realism. It is a diverse group that is risk averse, and likes to show and tell the stories of our turbulent world.

Next is Gen Alpha born between 2010 and 2025. These are the children who have been and will be immersed in technology their entire lives. They are also called the "Glass Generation," as glass-fronted devices will be their main medium of communication. They will take on jobs that don't even exist today. They will interact and play with AI and robots, and plan to visit Mars as a career goal. One can't help but wonder how the impact of the Corona Virus and the now inter-related global wars will leave its mark on them.

It is a gift to have knowledge, experience, and understanding of the impact the events had on what each generation lived through. It is essential we lean into what we can learn from one another, adjusting to the new and unknown at each juncture of change. Is it hard to see each other and respect one another? Yes. Is it worth it? Absolutely. We need each other's wisdom in our rapidly changing yet consistent world. Technology and connectivity have and will continue to change. Economy has always been and always will be up and down.

Love and war, between people and nations, has been a part of life on earth since humans said "yes" to our arch enemy. Yet, Salvation came and we can choose better. There is Hope. We can choose to respect our differences, learn, grow, and have stronger outcomes.

*I know of no single formula for success.
But over the years I have observed that some attributes of
leadership are universal and are often about finding ways of
encouraging people to combine their efforts, their talents, their
insights, their enthusiasm and their inspiration to work together.*
Queen Elizabeth II

Petite, confident and beautiful, she bounded onto the stage and spoke with excellence. I knew I had to connect with her and a few months later we had iced tea and a family lunch together. I listened with awe to this young woman and how she lives life to the fullest.

Victoria DiNatale

Bullied, But Not Beaten

My life weighed in the balance during my mom's pregnancy as she was airlifted from Savannah to Jacksonville during a hurricane watch. I arrived eleven weeks early, weighing only two pounds and ten ounces. My twin brother weighed a whole pound more at three pounds and ten ounces.

Public life began for me at age two, when my twin and I were featured on the front page of the Savannah Morning News while attending Memorial Hospital's Neonatal Intensive Care Nursery's Annual Valentine's Day Reunion. My mother continued her desire to give back to the community that had helped save our lives, and at times that put us kids in the spotlight. At age three, I was a calendar girl for Memorial Children's Hospital. As children, we were taught to learn, work, study, bring honor to our God and family, and give allegiance to the community in which we lived. These values are such an integral part of all that I am and all that I do.

We began learning good work ethic at an early age. We learned to work for what we wanted, and not to expect to be given these things. Being part of a working class family, Mom couldn't always pay for things we wanted, so we found contests to earn the needed money. I remember my brother wanting a Thomas the Tank Engine Halloween costume. Mom encouraged him to enter a coloring contest; the prize was $25. He won it, and with great joy bought his own costume.

My journey in the public eye continued. When I was five, WTOC-TV interviewed our family was interviewed during the Children's Miracle Network Telethon. My ten year-old sister, Leah, was inspired by us—her twin siblings—to design a t-shirt for the Children's Miracle Network. Her design was featured two babies with the slogan, "Life is a Miracle." She raised more than $10,000 from t-shirt sales. At one point, I was selected to be on the cover of Coastal Family Magazine. At thirteen, my brother and I had the privilege of painting the welcome greeting cards, which were placed on top of gift baskets for World Leaders attending the G8 Summit on Sea Island, Georgia.

My confident life took a turn at age eleven when I experienced bullying at school. At the beginning of middle school, a group of girls ganged up on me with severe bullying. They also began to actively recruited other students against me. As a result of the constant stress from the bullying, I developed a stress cough and Post Traumatic Stress Disorder.

That same year, Miss America 2003, Erika Harold, came to Savannah. Her platform was anti-bullying. I remember when she placed the Miss America crown on my head and told me to tell the other kids, "Miss America said that you better be nice to me.'" What an inspiration she was, giving me hope and a measure of courage. For my survival, my parents took me out of that middle school and placed me in another school. I was sick for two years, but with the help of my family, healthcare professionals and God, I overcame the trauma.

Despite all that was going on in my life, my family continued to give back to the community. The next big project we worked on, at age thirteen, was to help raise money for the Ronald McDonald House in Savannah. We wanted to help other parents who had premature or sick children. We designed and painted Christmas cards for the Ronald

McDonald House, which were sold to the public. The cards raised over $6,000 the first year.

As a freshman in high school, my contest entry was selected to be the theme for the Martin Luther King Junior Day Parade. I pitched the theme, "Dream, Believe, Achieve. Martin Luther King Jr. did."

After that, I had the joy of shadowing Senator Regina Thomas at the Georgia State Senate and watching other senators at work. My brother and I were recognized in the Georgia State Senate for high test scores, and in 2008 we were featured by WJCL News as Champions of Change for outstanding community service.

Some of the same bullies from middle school followed me to high school. They picked up where they left off before I swapped schools. This time, they used a new type of bullying—cyber bullying. The bullying became so severe I had to transfer high schools.

My whole traumatic experience in school led me to what I do now. I started going to schools, churches and the community to share the message that students can overcome bullying and be happy. I have spoken to thousands of parents, teachers and children across the region. God has affirmed me and given me the ability to speak before others and deliver my message of hope and help. In 2010, I had the privilege to address faith leaders at a Faith Leaders Seminar about how God pulled me through those horrific days. He truly does use everything for good in our lives if we let Him use us.

Being confident in your abilities can sometimes intimidate others, but I never allowed the bullies to change me. Because of my harsh childhood experiences, I developed a deep empathy for others. I believe in being kind and treating others as you want to be treated.

In our family, we were raised to support and love one another. We were never allowed to say hateful things or be unkind. I have experienced the joy and power of teaching these values to others.

I went on to college and earned my bachelor's degree in English. I became an anti-bullying motivational speaker, traveling extensively. I also became a columnist for the Savannah Morning News. My column, "Bullying Breakdown," was another venue I had to share the message of hope. I love to teach and have a deep spiritual connection to my work. I am passionate about empowering others to help change what is wrong in society.

I find deep fulfillment in mentoring young women who struggle with a lack of self-esteem. What was meant to hurt and harm me has turned to praise and thanksgiving by empowering others. What an honor, privilege and joy to be healed and used by God to help change the world, one girl at a time!

Victoria's powerful work continues. If you would like to know more about her, have her speak and touch your world, please go to: www.standingvictorious.com and www.facebook.com/standingvictorious

*How wonderful it is that nobody need wait
a single moment before starting to improve the world.*
Anne Frank

A warm welcome of joy wrapped around me as the sprightly four-foot-ten-inch Ms. Helen flung her door open to invite me in to her home. Her energy and smile filled the nautical-themed room where she made sure I had the most comfy chair and offered me a tall glass of iced tea. What she shared came smoothly and I knew that giving was as easy as breathing to her. Little did I know the depths her giving had reached.

Helen Campbell

Forgiving the Unthinkable

I was a thoroughbred New Yorker, transplanted to Savannah when my husband—who I met at age thirteen—moved here for work. I didn't like it! It was too hot, and there was no shopping! I was terribly verbal about my dislike. My husband, Bob, came home one night, sat me down and said, "You are making us all miserable with your complaining. Stop it."

I tried so hard to not complain and it worked! Bob and I have now been married fifty-one years and had three children, Richard, Susan and Charles. I grew to love beautiful Savannah. It has been such a blessing, even though I experienced the greatest trial of my life here.

My daughter Susan was dating a brilliant young man named Jody Ziglar. One morning, she left a note on her bed saying she was pregnant and that she and Jody had eloped. They had a daughter, and Jody took responsibility and went to work. Susan was expecting their second child when there was an industrial incident at Jody's job. A tire blew up in his face. He hung onto life, but died two weeks later. Their son was born two months after Jody's death.

After some time passed, our dentist wanted to set up a date with Susan and one of his patients. Finally, she agreed to go and the two eventually married. Unbeknown to me, her second husband was an extremely abusive man who put her in the hospital twelve times. He told her that if she told her parents what he was doing that he would kill her brothers.

Susan and her abusive husband started an electrical business and he built a large house. You couldn't see into the house, as it had a big fence around it. Susan fell pregnant with twins, and when they were about four months old, she called me in despair sharing that one of the babies was dead. I still had no idea what was happening in their home.

When their baby, Kimberley, was nine months old, Susan was upstairs working. Her husband called her to come down and bring him something. "I'll be there in a minute, just finishing up," she said. The next thing she knew, he came upstairs, grabbed her by her hair and dragged her downstairs. He then beat her with a piece of wood. Susan saw a gun lying on the washing machine. She grabbed it and killed her husband in self-defense.

The Judge didn't put her in jail, but he did restrict her. She couldn't vote, couldn't leave the city, and she needed to be home with the three children. She did all of that, and continued working in the electric business.

Susan had made some bad decisions. Now that I finally knew the truth of it all, I blamed myself. I believed if I had been more committed to God, I would have been a better mother.

Susan had a kind heart and sometimes had some of the kids from the trailer park over to her house for cookouts. One night, some of the boys from the trailer park tried to break into a house down the street from Susan's. The neighbor's alarm went off and the boys hid. The police drove by, yet saw nothing.

The boys then wondered around, and went into the convenience store where the police showed up. They waited for the cops to leave and decided to go to Susan's place next. First, they disconnected the wiring from the outside wooden utility house. When her dogs started barking, they killed them. Susan had no hearing in one ear—due to her ex hitting her so hard and damaging it, so she didn't hear anything.

The boys went to my granddaughter Kimberley's room, and started beating her. She screamed before they knocked her out. Susan heard her and came running in bewilderment. The boys had knives and lunged toward Susan, stabbing her. One boy commented about how nauseous he became, as he didn't know it took so long to kill someone. He then slit Susan's throat and she died. All of these details were proudly shared during the trials to come.

After they killed Susan, then took Kimberley upstairs, raped her, stabbed her, beat her, and threw her body aside. They took gasoline and matches and set the house alight. The house burned to the ground.

The next day, the boys stood across from the house and next to the cops asking questions. They had stolen Kimberley's boom box, some oxycodone pills, and some cheap St. Patty's day jewelry. The boys weren't on drugs. At first they were only going to break in, just to steal a few things. But Satan entered the scene. One boy said, "I can't do this." The other responded, "Oh, you are. You're finishing this with me."

That was nineteen years ago. Later, an autopsy revealed that Kimberley was alive when she was burned to death. Susan was forty-three and Kimberley thirteen when they were killed. The trauma of my daughter and granddaughter's murders has been the trial of my life. I've had to lean on God every day. Psalm 119:71 has become my life verse. *"The Lord allows these things to happen so I can learn His decrees."*

I was not close to God when all of this happened. I had been a part of many different Christian denominations—Catholic, Lutheran, Methodist. Now, I know Jesus and the difference between religion and relationship. I know Jesus says I need to love, love everybody above everything. I do love Him and appreciate the difficulties which bring me closer to Him. I have learned to understand what He means when He says that we need to forgive.

Forgiveness is the hardest thing to do. During the second trial of the young men, I kept praying to The Lord, "Holy Spirit, make me accept what God said that I am to forgive." Through prayer and spending time at church and worship, I finally said, "I can do this with your help."

About two years after the murders, I decided to write to the boys in prison. I spoke to them about Jesus who loves them and that shared that He asks us to forgive. "I pray each day that He will help me forgive you. I hate what you did, but I do not hate you. Boys, look Jesus in the eye and tell Him you're sorry, ask forgiveness and accept Him."

My son Richard asked how I could forgive those kids. All I can say is that the act of forgiveness is between God and me. I have seen the spiritual need to forgive these boys. God uses my forgiving to help me get through each day. Eventually, Richard asked if we could pray together. We did. "There it is, Mom," he said. We hugged and have grown closer than ever. A few years ago, he and his wife went to church and responded to the call to baptism.

My husband died four years after Susan and Kimberly's deaths. He didn't do well with it all. He changed, became withdrawn. Thankfully, he was at peace at the end.

I have had to accept that you can't live in the past. I continue to ask God to keep me strong and to stay in His presence. If I let go of His presence, the resentment can easily resurface.

Jesus walks with me each morning. I spend my days in joy, with my sweet doggy by my side. Three things are important in my life: humility, patience, and faith.

I have learned:

To have faith in all God's promises.

God has my best interest at heart.

Don't look back.

God doesn't ask us to do more than what He has done for us. He is there all the time. Just ask Him to go with you every day, step-by-step. He is a loving God with a good sense of humor. He can't help unless we ask Him. We need to have faith if we are to do what He has for us to do. It is good to be afflicted and to learn His decrees.

Hear what God is saying to you. Open your heart and let the Holy Spirit in. He came and said, "We must forgive others and He will forgive us." Whatever difficulty you're having is difficult to your offender too. Humble yourself and go along with what Jesus has to say.

Helen Campbell is retired and lives on Wilmington Island, Georgia. She serves others by volunteering for The Ronald McDonald House Charities. She knits with the Friends 'n' Needles group at Isle Of Hope Methodist Church where she is also a greeter. She volunteers to clean communion trays and is part of the Emmaus community. She speaks for Jesus whenever asked.

I can do all things through Christ who strengthens me.
Paul, the Apostle in Philippians 4:13

PART FOUR

Together We Are Stronger

Because of Gender

Together We Are Stronger
Because of Gender

From the simplicity of the physical genders being male and female, gender identity and expression has become a complex issue. No longer is gender about anatomy, but about who each person sees themselves to be. Currently there are about 64 terms that describe gender identity and expression, if you'd like to know more, do take a look at them online. There are many sites with information available, such as HealthLine.com. You can find various research and opinions related to nature, nurture, experiences, DNA, and all that makes us who we are, or choose to be, in the realm of gender.

From the Biblical perspective it is clear, God made humankind in His image, male and female. He made men and women for one another, to love each other, to procreate together, have sex with, and to cherish and live life together. One man and one woman, in one marriage, till death do they part. This is the plan the enemy has fouled up. Divorce has become standard, living together outside of marriage commonplace, and the many gender identity and expressions have no place for the simplicity of two God-created genders—him and her, male and female.

Differences in gender identity evoke much emotion, bias, prejudice and intolerance of one another, especially in the religious world. People have been thrown out, abandoned, even stoned, for identifying differently—just as it once was for diversity of color, origin, making bad choices such as committing a grievous crime, or even just for being a less "desirable" sex in a particular culture.

It is no secret that women have suffered awful injustices, have fought hard against them for freedom, have won some battles, and yet still fight for total respect and equality without abuse. As we struggle for our rights in the Western world it is hard to think that there are still places on earth where women have no rights and are treated as second class. Fighting for equal rights is essential. No person, whether male or female, or any other gender identification, should be treated as "less than." We are all human beings on this earth together.

No matter what your belief system is, there is no place for disrespect, judgment or ill-mannered behavior toward people who are different from you. Whether you believe in the one-man-and-one-woman forever-marriage, or whether you do not. We are all commissioned to "love one another" (John 13:34). Love one another—PERIOD. That's it. Our challenge is to ensure that our hearts don't harbor secret anger, hate, or disgust while striving to love everyone with God's love.

If gender identity and expression is one of the differences you feel strongly about, the answer is still the same. It's simple: love one another. Look at your deepest emotion and see the root of your prejudice and bias. Learn how to love when it is hard to do.

Together we must learn how to compose differences, not with arms, but with intellect and decent purpose.
Dwight D. Eisenhower

I took a hurried last sip of my iced tea after Jenny Lynn Anderson's keynote speech for the Women Alumni of Georgia Southern University. The atmosphere around us was dense with passion. You could feel the intensity and conviction that enraptured the audience as courage poured through Jenny Lynn's story.

Jenny Lynn had first shared her story only nine months prior, but she'd carried it within her for twenty years. Every word was powerful and mingled with delicateness. Her innate ability to focus on the good would, one day, be the driving force in keeping her faith, her mind, and her sanity intact.

Jenny Lynn Anderson

From Complex Quietude to Outspoken Survivor

My husband, two precious daughters, and I moved back to Statesboro, Georgia where I grew up. My childhood was fairly easy with no huge trials. The hardest thing I had ever experienced was dealing with my mom's drinking. Her social drinking turned into alcoholism when I was in college. My mom is a strong woman and was the first female judge in Georgia. She sought treatment for her addiction, and it saved her life. I didn't realize how much her addiction affected me at the time, but seeing her go through that battle with alcohol made me self-reliant and determined to be independent.

After my family and I settled back in Statesboro, I began working in the Public Relations department of an alcohol and drug treatment hospital. Within the first ninety days, I was asked to go to Atlanta for a convention. I was so excited. I arrived in Atlanta and pitched a story idea for our hospital's magazine. I decided I would go in to the city and look around for a bit, so I went upstairs to my room to freshen up and change.

As I opened my door to exit my hotel room, I saw a man coming toward me. He grabbed a hold of my arm, pulled a knife out, and began dragging me back into my room. I screamed and fought him to try to get away. The man put his knife to my throat and threatened to kill me if I didn't stop screaming. I felt stuck. I wanted to continue fighting him with everything I had, but I didn't want to die.

Once he was assured that I would stop screaming, my attacker ripped the phone out of wall and said, "I'm going to rape you." I did what I later learned was the last thing a victim in my situation should do; I begged him not to rape me. I gave him my money, my credit cards, and jewelry. In a frantic state of trying to control even just one aspect of my situation, I decided I couldn't allow him to see my wedding ring. I turned my ring around so that he couldn't see the stone.

I had never been involved in anything violent in my life. I was petrified and absolutely traumatized. He put the knife to my neck once again and commanded me, "Take off your clothes." I still didn't want him to see my ring. I kept hiding it. I clung to it. He then performed oral sex on me and disrobed me leaving my bra still on. I knew I needed to get out. I felt that if I didn't leave he was going to kill me.

Think, think, think! What can I do? I tried to dissuade him from his plan by saying, "My boss is coming to get me any minute." He went to the bathroom for a washcloth, and I wondered what that could possibly be for. I knew something bad was going to happen. I looked at the door and then looked at him as I half-screamed, "Don't you hear him coming? He's going to get you!"

He got off the bed and cracked the door. I saw a housekeeper through the crack and screamed so loudly that people came out of their rooms. My attacker flew out the door, past the housekeeper, and down the emergency staircase. He was gone. They never caught him, but I know that God had sent an angel in the form of a housekeeper to save my life.

The hotel security didn't call the police when I notified them of my attack. I found out later that people had heard me scream and came out of their rooms to see what happened, but all they saw was a black leather jacket going into the room. Yet no one called the police, and that added to my trauma. Finally, I made my way to the police precinct. The hardest thing I had to do was call my husband and tell him what happened.

After that, I went to stay the night with a friend in Atlanta, as I refused to return to the hotel. At four o'clock that morning, I woke up in a rage. I felt that women needed to know about what happened. I called my media contacts and they interviewed me. Later, my mom and my husband came. My mama, thinking like a lawyer, asked me, "Jenny Lynn, are you sure you want to do this?"

I decided that I was making decisions out of anger, and not out of concern for others, so I canceled the rest of the interviews. That was the moment I changed forever. I never again would look in the mirror and see the strong, independent woman I once was.

I went back to my hometown and learned the devastating fact that our culture silences women on topics such as rape. It's just too horrible, so you're not supposed to talk about it. Contrary to who I was in my heart, I stayed silent.

I functioned as well as I could and raised my two beautiful girls. My husband and I built and opened funeral homes as our business. I did what I loved through marketing and public relations. Yet, inside I knew I had changed and had lost self-confidence. Deep down, I experienced terror and chronic fear.

I looked for my attacker in every man I saw, always thinking that he would come back and finish what he started. Post Traumatic Stress set in and I began to have a panic attack if a man even walked toward me. I never became "used to it." I never "got over it." Fear traumatized me afresh every time thoughts of my attack surfaced. I have since wondered if my physical heart has been damaged through all the years of fear and high levels of untreated cortisol.

Unbeknown to me, depression began to take over my life. I had never been a sad or easily upset person, but my attacker had me in shackles long after his fingerprints left my skin. I was held hostage for years after I left that room.

People around me had no idea the condition I was in and I knew that they wouldn't understand, couldn't understand. I chose to remain silent and move on with my life the best way I could, but I was dying inside. I so wanted to be that young, vivacious woman that once had great dreams. I knew she was somewhere inside of me still, but I couldn't resurrect Jenny Lynn until God became involved.

God had me on His radar long before that horrible day, even though I had walked away from Him at an early age. As a young child, I remember attending church for a while, but my dad never went. My mother made the effort to attend for a few years before we all quit going. There was no great foundation of God in my life.

After the traumatic experience in Atlanta, I was broken. I learned that my family and closest friends couldn't fix me. Finally, I started attending a Bible study and went to church where I proceeded to cry my eyes out. I knew God was the only one who could help me.

The only times I felt relief from any of my circumstances were the brief times I spent in God's presence. He calmed me in those moments. I had to take baby steps to learn about God, as I knew nothing. As I became more involved, I had personal experiences with Him and realized that He was my best friend and would never leave me. Coming to know God as my best friend and safe place was the beginning of my healing.

In 1999, I experienced a pivotal changing point during a Beth Moore Bible study. God revealed to me that the only way I could fully heal was to forgive my attacker. I obeyed. I didn't know his name or where he was, but I still had the police sketch.

I avoided looking at the police sketch of my attacker's face because it hurt so much to remember it all. That day, after the Bible study, I pulled out the sketch of the man who haunted me. For the first time, I felt sorry for him. I knew he wasn't raised like I was. He must have been raised in brutality, and hurt me because he had been hurt. I forgave him and took my first of many small steps forward toward healing and restoration. I felt as if my life was being restored somewhat, but it took me another ten years before I finally went to counseling.

Even though I was making steps in my healing process, I was still experiencing panic attacks. Night terrors became a regular occurrence and when my husband would come to bed late, I'd scream, lash out, and wake up. One night, during a panic attack, I woke up not knowing what was happening. My Post Traumatic Stress was accelerating and the trauma was on replay in my subconscious. I had no awareness and no control over my reactions.

I called my sister, who once again lovingly told me, "You need to get some help." I went to a psychologist who started working with me using cognitive therapy. I faithfully completed my homework, but I didn't see any marked improvement. The best way I can describe what I was dealing with is that it was similar to what soldiers experience after returning home from war. I have never been to war, but I know what being at war with my mind is like.

During the time I was seeing the psychologist, I had coffee with my mentor and began exploring what I wanted to do with the rest of my life. I had put my life and dreams on hold for so long, and always said I was "fine." My mentor saw through my facade and asked how I was dealing with the assault I had experienced.

He then said, "I always thought you had a greater story to tell." The minute he said it, something washed over me. Three days later, the pressure continued to weigh on me and I knew I had a story others needed to hear. I battled within myself knowing that sharing my story was what God wanted me to do with my life. My spirit cried out, "No not that story!" The Spirit sweetly answered, "Yes, that's the story I need you to tell." That's when I began writing my book.

No one ever approached me or offered to help me through the lonely years after my attack. Now, women come to me and I can tell them that there is help. There is hope. As sexual assault rape victims, no one speaks or shouts for your voice to be heard. There are no marches for our cause. Victims become survivors.

In my experience, I have learned that until we as victims become transparent, we will never heal. Sharing our stories is the piece that sets us free. I am free now, and it feels so good. I didn't believe I could ever experience this kind of emotional and spiritual freedom again. I was an optimist, but during my dark years, I still couldn't believe I could truly be happy again. What I didn't realize in my self-evaluation was that God didn't want the old Jenny Lynn back. He wanted a new, better one. He promised He could use my ugly story for good if I would give Him the ashes, and He has done just that.

I live my life and feel alive in it now. I cannot believe the doors that have opened. I have a deep desire for women and men to heal from all of the hidden wounds in their lives. Women speak to me about rape, and men come to me about molestation. My sharing my story empowers them to start on the path to healing.

People—survivors—carry such shame about enduring sexual attacks. Through my journey, I became adamant about the fact that I didn't want the label "Sexual Assault Victim." I am a "Sexual Assault Survivor." I am not a victim who is merely managing life; I live life with purpose now. I have learned that until you can feel, you cannot heal, and I choose healing even if it hurts. I'm a survivor.

My hands caress the cover of Jenny Lynn's book, titled **Room 939**. *My soul is deeply stirred and quiet. A tear trickles down my cheek. I don't think I will ever be the same again.*

Jenny Lynn Anderson's book **Room 939** *includes 6 QR codes readers can scan, which leads them to a sound bite of music that creates the emotional backdrop of the story. Reading her book is a stirring and emotional experience.*

Jenny Lynn speaks and teaches wherever she can. To read more of her story, purchase her book, or invite her to speak to your group, visit: www.jennylynnanderson.com

Together we can face any challenges
as deep as the ocean and as high as the sky.
Sonia Gandhi

We met at my Emmaus weekend retreat. Sarah was serving with energy and having fun. I felt so relaxed with her humor and positivity filling the air with smiles. We then served at the Lead n Link Conference together, where her skills and giving were so clearly seen on all she touched. It was clear, she is no everyday woman. Each time we meet, she shares more of her story and who she is. Hearing what God has done in her and through her makes my heart expand with wonder.

Sarah Williams

Storms and Peace

I love family! My family is my joy. They are my dream come true—a dream which seemed to elude me as I longed for a family of my own for many years. Growing up, I had no roots. We always moved from place to place as my dad received business promotions. My younger brother and I had an "oh-so-different" school-teacher, our mom. She wasn't like other moms. It was hard to please her and, try as I may, I couldn't. She made it clear that when I was done with college, I was on my own.

With little confidence, I headed off to college and met the cutest boy! He filled the gaps in each corner of my being and we soon married. He and I had two children, and they were enough for me. I was determined to give our children all I longed for in life, yet, before I knew it, my husband and I divorced and the dream was over. In a feeble attempt to numb the pain of the experience, I rebounded and started dating the typical "bad boy," who was also abusive.

A little while later, my ex-husband found God. He called me and said, "I'm praying for you." My reply was bitter and angry as I blurted back, "I don't want your prayers." I don't remember ever going to church. I didn't know God, or anything about the Bible at all. By that time, I was caught up in a horrible, abusive relationship that was like a bad movie. I honestly didn't think God would want me, and didn't feel good enough for Him. During it all, my awesome girlfriends invited me to their church and I joined an all-women's class where I soon discovered who Jesus was.

I decided to marry the man I was seeing and brought my precious children into the abusive relationship. Six weeks later, I knew if I didn't get out I would die. Petrified, I prayed, "God, I have to get out of this. I don't want to die. I promise I will raise my children with You." At that moment, the presence of God was with me, and two angels walked me and my children out of the relationship and situation.

Divorced for the second time, I moved to Knoxville to open a new bank. I also met a new man. We married and moved to Savannah to join my dad in his new business venture. I hoped we could begin a smooth life with the children. We were going to church, but my relationship with Jesus was not real or daily in my life at that time. We had another child and our issues grew into insurmountable obstacles, leaving me at the end of my third marriage and facing another divorce. I was finally at the point I decided I was ready to raise my three children with God.

A few years later, I was set up on a blind date. We both had been through a lot, yet were compatible. We dated for a year as we got to know Jesus. We both felt we were not worthy enough to remarry. Then, we went on the Emmaus retreat and we realized God loved us as we were.

We married with a new sense of freedom in the joy of Jesus who forgives and heals. Along the way, I learned God must come first if I wanted a successful marriage. We started praying for our ex-spouses. I called my ex-husband, and asked for forgiveness. Each of us poured our hearts into prayer and now we and all our ex-spouses get along.

We told our children how much we deeply loved them. We wanted the children to know that adults make mistakes, need forgiveness, and must forgive. Our children are integrated.

My husband and I love each one of them, regardless of who their biological parents are. The children and the adults in our pieced-together family have loving relationships. We are one huge extended family, related through the multiplicity of marriages. The most important part we emphasize is for each person to know unconditional love.

Only a miracle of God could bring such healing and restoration. I always said I wanted a family. God did not just give me a family, He gave me an extended family. We now live with my dad. We moved in to help with my mom who had developed Alzheimer's, and continued to stay there after she was laid to rest. I truly enjoy a huge family. It's great knowing we are all here for one another.

When my husband became ill a few years ago, the first thing our family did was pray. We didn't panic, but instead we cried and gave it to Jesus. I thought I would be my husband's caregiver, but soon realized I didn't have the strength. I broke down a few times, but received a great sense of calm when I realized even Jesus had tears. Through prayer and counsel, God assured me He wouldn't ask for more of me than I could give. He only wanted me to be His hands and feet and do the best I could on any given day.

I'm happy to say God brought my husband through cancer! Once again, we have the joy of more time together, doing the things we love, like reading together. We pray every night for each of our family members, and we are all closer to Jesus than we have ever been before.

A couple of years ago, my eldest son shared he was gay. At first, his dad had a hard time accepting him, so we began to pray. One day, his dad called and we cried when we heard him say, "I love you; you're my son." Our family doesn't turn on each other when times are tough, or when things don't turn out as we think they should. We accept each other and love each other through everything that comes.

Looking back to when my son was younger, there were signs of homosexuality then. When he was in high school, he was mortified over it and felt doomed. He tried having a relationship with a girl, but ended up breaking her heart. He felt it was not fair to pretend if he couldn't love her the way she needed love. It was hard to watch my child struggle with sexuality and my heart broke.

My entire being shuddered when he shared about walking home from the library one evening in Washington, DC. A group of teenage boys, unknown to him, started following him and began stoning him, crying out, "Fagot, fagot!" They hurled one stone after another until he finally reached safety.

As a Christian mother, I had to come to terms with my son's sexuality. I have wrestled with what my friends say, and with what the Bible says. Finally, I heard God say, "Love one another. Don't judge." I looked at my own life. I was married and divorced three times. God loved me, and people loved me and didn't judge me for my life. I looked at people who have all kinds of struggles: gluttony, anger, sexual acting out, criminal pasts. "Love them; don't judge," is all I hear God say.

My son loves Jesus and is active in his church. He tithes and makes a difference in the community. He is a strong, independent, brave young man. "Mom, you have never had to fight for rights, or to be accepted. It's tough. I'm human; just like you."

He is a loving human being, who at age eighteen, went to Israel to work with Arab children. He would pick them up and take them for heart transplants, serving the Lord, and working on his personal relationship with God.

I have three sons, one gay, two straight, and they all love Jesus. I would rather have my sons loving Jesus than anything else in the world.

I still have questions. Questions like, does loving Jesus make homosexuality right or wrong? Did my son choose his lifestyle? How do I deal with it? The only answer I have is, "Love; don't judge."

I love my son through everything, absolutely and definitely. I know God gave me my sons for me to love them, and to teach them about Jesus. They are His to work in and through. Jesus is the only one who can lead them through their struggles and situations. I will never abandon or reject them.

Though my children are grown, my work with kids continues. I teach high schoolers who don't have families about Jesus. Our home is a place they can come to experience a loving family. They can come over, swim, eat, or just talk at our kitchen table. God gave me a heart for kids, and each one who enters our home becomes extended family. I've learned if I do what God asks and love like He loves, I am blessed with the love children give to me. My bounty is full and rich.

I love my family. God truly is an extravagant God! My relationship with Him continues to grow and expand. My thanks and praise overflow! I am excited about the future of my entire family!

To connect with Sarah, email her at sarah@lbfarm.net.

> *The greatest gift you can give to others is the gift of unconditional love and acceptance.*
> Brian Tracy

PART FIVE

Together We Are Stronger

Because of Socio-Economic Standing

Together We Are Stronger
Because of Socio-Economic Standing

History indicates that there have always been the "Have's" and the "Have-Not's." The wealthy and the poor. As a little girl, my heart was crushed when seeing the haunted eyes, and snot dripping over the crusted upper lip of filthy, dirty, shoe-less people. Then a smell I couldn't name would hit me. It took many years for me to learn that these people were poor, and many more years to realize the varied levels of poverty.

I stood aghast the first time I visited New York City and saw extreme poverty alongside untold wealth. The one tripping over the other—seemingly unseen. How could it be? How can we literally walk over or bump shoulders with one another and not care? How can we eradicate poverty? Can we?

There are a few places on this earth that have minimized extreme poverty, whilst in others it expands. The United Nations World Summit identified poverty eradication as an ethical, social, economic, and political imperative of mankind and has called on governments to address root causes of poverty, provide for basic needs for all, and ensure the poor have access to productive resources, including credit, training and education. What would the world be like if we could ALL do this!

The truth is as this sobering Scripture says, "The poor you will always have with you,"(Matthew 26:11 NIV). "If there is among you a poor man of your brethren, within any of the gates in your land which the Lord your God is giving you,

you shall not harden your heart nor shut your hand from your poor brother, but you shall open your hand wide to him and willingly lend him sufficient for his need, whatever he needs," (Deuteronomy 15: 7, 8 -11 NKJV).

The extreme divide between the wealthy and poor is marked, yet there is a subtle divide in-between. It resides in the places where children, teenagers, and adults in their various neighborhoods gain status through brands of clothing, expensive cars, and travel opportunities. Pretense can be upheld through filtered pictures and selfies on social media. Here too, the subtle hand of separation sneaks in through who owns the latest technology device, and declaring statuses with picture-perfect posts. Perhaps the future of AI and tech communication may remove this layer of separation, or will it add to it?

Perhaps as we continue to focus on personal growth, self-worth, purposeful living, owning our God-given talents, and skill-set development, we can find hope. Combined with caring for one another better, respecting each other, and learning what true love is, the human race can survive.

One story at a time, we can win.

It's going to take a movement, a massive army to achieve breaking down the walls created by socio-economic status.

I am in!

Are you?

Coming together is a beginning;
keeping together is progress;
working together is success.
Henry Ford

We met when Open Hearts Shelter in Statesboro, GA was still just a shell. She stepped into the unfinished room looking like a glamor model, confident, yet demure, with an inner strength that beckoned me to get to know her. I hadn't quite seen a Pastor's wife like her. She was that AND as I've come to know, she is a Pastor, a gifted singer, speaker, prayer warrior that God uses mightily.

Janet Swanson

One Voice with Global Impact

    I was a Daddy's girl. I came out of the womb "his." I was a singer and full of personality. I was even paid to sing. I was independent, strong-willed, and didn't need people. I was just like my dad and he favored me.

    Dad was minister, but he was also abusive to my mother and brothers. He never hit me. I sensed my mother didn't like me, and felt she didn't love me. I loved her deeply, yet felt so unloved by her. I was six when they divorced and I lived with my mom.

    Being hungry a lot, Mother looked for a provider who could help take care of us. She married a man who was an alcoholic. He was an angry man who abused my brothers and sexually abused me. The attention started in the shower. As it continued getting worse, I knew he would rape me if I didn't do something. I was 10-years-old, going to school each day, living life, and barely surviving.

    I wanted to suicide, and decided to do so. It was dark in the room. I was praying, crying, asking God to do it for me. I was determined to get out of my horrible life. My way out was to die. I didn't go to church anymore, even though Daddy was still a preacher. I remembered God was out there and that He could hear me.

    Right before I took the pills, I laid down on my bed and God came to me in a very real way. There was a vivid sound in the wall. It moved around and when I went to the window to look, there was the moon, filled with glory and so close.

As I looked up, I felt warmth and hope come upon me. Hope rose up inside me, and I felt as if I were floating back to my bed. The presence of love and power filled me. I heard God's voice say, "Don't kill yourself. In the morning when you wake up, you will get help. You will tell somebody."

I woke up the next morning and was bold enough to tell someone the truth of what was happening to me.

Mother had a decision to make, leave her new husband and save me, or stay with him and give me up. She stayed with him, choosing to give me up. It was so painful. I went to foster care, overcome with grief. After a year, Daddy came and rescued me and I stayed with him. My journey was dark from age 12 to 17. I began acting promiscuously to cover up my pain. I laughed a lot in public, and cried a lot in private

The first time I was invited to church and went, I felt the same presence of God I felt that day in my room. I gave my heart to the Lord that day. Salvation was instant, but healing came in time. Little did I know that my husband to be was leading worship the day I found the Lord.

I lost both of my parents when I was in my 30's. God allowed many emotions to resurface at that time, which led me to deeper healing from the cobwebs in my heart that still haunted me. There were many things I had hidden in my heart that I never understood until the abundance of Jesus dealt with it.

Now I tell people how powerful Jesus is to heal. If He can heal me after all I went through, He can do it for you. He is a healer. He is not angry. He is not mad. He is kind, compassionate, and intentional. He is in love with me. Jesus loves me. And He loves you.

Healing is a process. Though I had been leading worship and preaching, I found myself once again in a very dark place.

God gently showed me idols I had in my life—one being the need for affirmation. Oh, how I needed people's affirmation!

In the midst of my inner healing process, as I sat on the edge of my bed, missing my Daddy, I looked over and saw his guitar. I asked, "Where are you God?"

In response, God didn't condemn me for being where I was at. Instead, He addressed my intention to be more for Him. God whispered, "Pick up the guitar."

I thought, "No, I can't even play a cord."

Again I heard the voice, "Pick it up."

I picked up the guitar and—miraculously—I could play. Sound came out. I was amazed. I received a supernatural ability to learn. I went on YouTube, learned more, listened, made a sound. Two weeks later, I was playing the guitar at a church service.

Years before God gave me this special gift, my husband and I went into music ministry. We were like Aaron and Moses. Moses couldn't speak, but Aaron could. My husband couldn't play an instrument or read music, but I could. I did all the behind the scenes work and for seven years we served in this way.

One day, a doctor told me I couldn't have kids. For one week, I prayed, asking to have children. I claimed the promise as I prayed, "You said, if I delight myself in You, You will give me the desire of my heart." By faith I put baby booties by my bed and printed out adoption paperwork.

Within three months I was pregnant with our first son. I continued to live by faith, making steps to manifest faith in the God of miracles. God showed up, and we now have the joy of three strong young men of God.

My husband felt we needed to move back to Statesboro, Georgia, where two positions were open—Associate Pastor and

Worship Leader. I had never served while holding a title, but God assured me He would help me. God gave me a platform to do what was in my heart. I started writing songs, creating parts, and had so much fun living to worship the Lord!

Thirteen years into our marriage, God addressed my heart and not my behavior. Then He sent me on a journey of love. He taught me how to love my husband and my kids. It was a journey that will never end, learning to truly love. I felt nudges to tell people my story, but I felt shameful and afraid to do so. I would tell my story now and then without question in obedience as God instructed.

In my journey, God gave me a spiritual father who I could share my story with. That is when grief began to surface. When my father died, three years of darkness overcame me. I felt like that little girl in foster care. I knew God asked me to tell my story, but I was afraid. I started going to Christian counseling, which prevented the enemy from taking my life.

On New Year's Eve, I heard God saying, "You need to start writing your book tomorrow. Get up three hours before sunrise and I will instruct you how to do this." I got up and felt His breath on my neck and He said, "Write the table of contents. Now tell the story from the very beginning."

Every morning, I woke up early and wrote for three hours, crying all the way through. God was with me. I had a goal to finish writing by the end of November. It was a crazy busy time. We moved three times and our eldest son went to college. In the middle of writing the book, I quit. Our house was upside down as the water pipes had burst.

"Why would you tell me to write a book when all this mess is happening?" I questioned God.

During one service, I shared about my writing process. There was a new lady that was visiting the service that day, and when I mentioned my book she suddenly got up and quickly left, but she came back. As it turns out, she was so moved when she heard I was writing a book she had to walk out. She just so happened to be an editor and an author for a Chicken Soup for the Soul book.

"I will edit your book for free and I will pay for the publishing," she said to me after the services. "I will help you finish this book!"

I would speak and I would type, and she edited as we went along. We finished that book in November. God miraculously brought it all together.

Adriana, our band director, told me I need to make a CD. "The world needs to hear your voice," she said. She had written a few songs in Spanish and I knew I had to sing them and make a CD. God said to my heart, "Do this now."

It was January. I had been writing songs and we started recording. I became very ill, with pneumonia and lost my voice. Every Monday, Adriana and I came together to record. I'd say, "God, I can't do this today."

And He would respond, "Go and do it."

"I'm sick," I argued.

"I'll heal you when you get there," He countered.

My voice would be bad, but each time I obeyed, my voice would come back for the moment it was needed. Then it would leave again. It hurt. Then I would go into prayer asking God to heal the pain.

The CD we recorded is full of songs about healing and prayers for the broken hearted. The music recognizes the darkness and hurt of life, and the hope we can find in God. Those prayers were real, from the depths of my soul. God showed me that weeping endures for the night, but joy comes in the morning. The people I share my music with have become my "joy in the morning."

God said He will put me before prominent people—not just women—but children, schools, and universities to speak hope and healing. It happened. I speak about suicide, ways to escape, and how to get out. I liberally share, "There's a Healer waiting for you, a loving God."

Even when I can't share Jesus in the schools, I can give my book away. Talk about how to make lemonade out of lemons! He always makes something beautiful out of our ashes if we let Him. What a gracious, kind, miracle working God!

For more about Janet and to connect with her, subscribe to her podcast, One Voice. To purchase her book, **A Throne Room View**, *go to www.janetswansonministries.com.*

It only takes one voice, at the right pitch, to start and avalanche.
Dianna Hardy

I was inexplicably drawn to Georgette in what can only be a Holy Spirit collaboration. Beneath her quiet, sweet smile and laughing eyes lies a well of strength and fortitude. She has "compassion followed by action" for the homeless. We share the passion to give HOPE to the hopeless. She endlessly gives, even as the storms of life rage about her. Her courage and commitment to God so inspires me.

Georgette Jackson

Upheld and Holding Up

We were a happy family who lived in an old shack in Savannah, Georgia. We had an outside bathroom and had to use a hand-pump to get water. We were the last ones on our street to have running water put in, which happened when I was in high school! My single mom was a domestic and knew how to stretch the little money she made. I never felt poor because she would make us the finest clothes from the fabrics she bought.

We were, however, very poor and my mom, two sisters, grandparents, three uncles, and an aunt lived together. Our family was a mix of Christian denominations: Methodist, Pentecostal, and Baptist and I'd go from one church to the other with various family members.

When I was in the fifth grade, schools integrated for the first time. My first friend was a white girl and we stuck together, so I barely noticed the change at school. When high school came along, we were bussed to what previously was the all-white school. At times, there were a few problems on the school bus, but I can say I have never felt in danger or experienced real racial tension with anyone as a child or as an adult.

At age 17, I had completed all of the required school credits and could graduate from school three months early. It seemed that was God's plan, because during that time one of my aunts passed away birthing her seventh child. As if God worked it out, I moved in to take care of the kids while my uncle went to work. I cleaned and took care of kids while one of my cousins did the cooking.

The arrangement was a good thing for my uncle, but not for me. I met a boy, and he'd come over to the house. I became pregnant in March, officially graduated high school in June, and gave birth to my first daughter, Char, in December. What a year! After that, my uncle found a girlfriend, and my cousin and I moved back into our homes.

During my first year of college, I became pregnant with my second daughter, Dee. I duly left college after one year to get a job to help my mom provide for my daughters. My daughter's father married someone else, but a year later he was divorced, moved back to his mom's house and became sick.

I was close friends with his mom, so I went over to help take care of him during his illness. That brought our relationship back. We moved in together, and I became pregnant with my third child. I was so excited because it was a boy! I had so wanted a little boy.

I doted on my little boy! When he was three months old, I laid him in his crib to sleep. I went to check on him in the middle of the night, and he was still and cold. Just like that, he was gone with Sudden Infant Death Syndrome.

It was my first experience losing a child to death. Seeing his body lifeless practically destroyed me. God gave me a son, but not for long. Depression overtook me. Why did God give me a son and then take him? My faith wasn't strong at that time, so I pulled even further away from God and I stopped going to church. Thankfully, over time, I found my way back to the Lord.

Over the years, I became stronger as a woman and bold in my faith in Christ. I knew I had more to offer this world other than being a wife and mother. Although my marriage was on shaky ground for various reasons, I stayed in the relationship to keep my family together because that's what I saw the women in my family do; they stayed no matter what.

My girls grew up and had their own lives, so I felt it was time for me to end our facade of a marriage. I filed for divorce after separating from my husband for a short period of time.

Months later, working at the Savannah Board of Realtors, I received a call from my youngest daughter saying they had lost their home. I heard the Holy Spirit tell me to have their family of four come and live with me. Once again, my home was busy, filled with family, and my heart was full and restored.

I decided to go on a 21-day Daniel Fast. During that time, my prayer to the Lord was, "What is Your purpose for my life? What did You place me here for? What can I do to glorify You?"

I felt I needed to do more than just work at my great paying job. One night, I came home from work and turned on the TV. I watched the news story about a house for women in need. The house had closed and the women were turned out with nowhere to go. I fell to my knees and sobbed. It hurt my heart so. I didn't understand the intensity I had in my soul. It was if these women were my friends.

That night, I had a dream that I was to help homeless women. The Lord said to me, "Let them know I love them and I have not forgotten them. Take the love you have in your heart and pour it out on these women. You need Divine rest too; I will give it to you, and you bring My rest to them."

The scripture Matthew 11:28 echoed in my soul. "Come to Me, all who are weary and heavy laden, and I will give you rest."

The very next day, I went to work overwhelmed with my God-experience fresh on my mind. My heart ached, saying, "I don't know how to do this."

As I sat at work, Yvonne, a Realtor I hadn't seen in some time, walked in. The first thing she said was, "God sent me to see you, and for me to ask you what He told you last night."

I told her about my dream. She told me to take a pen and paper, and to write down some names she would tell me. She gave me a list of several people and told me to call them.

I was so green I didn't know what to do, so she told me each next step I was to take. Now, I was really overwhelmed! I'm the kind of person who likes to stay in the background, and I'm not very talkative. Calling that list of people was out of my comfort zone.

One of the people she told me to call answered and then asked me to call back on his other line. I had no intention of calling him back and didn't. Would you know, he called me back! He must have taken my number off of his phone, as I hadn't shared it with him.

He promptly told me to come by his office that day. God knew I would have waited, and eventually put off visiting because I was petrified. But when he told me to come that day, I went.

At our meeting, he asked, "Do you have any money?"

"No, not a dime, Sir."

He paid the fee for the 501(C3) non-profit status and told me to pay him back when I could. Before I knew it, all the Realtors pooled their money to pay for the fee, and I paid the man back. Everything happened so rapidly. God had it all set up.

I felt God tell me to go under the bridges and find the people. I felt I needed to take bottled water to the women.

The water would meet an essential need and provide the way to share Jesus' rest and love with them. I sent an email out to the Realtors and told them the plan. A few months later, we started going out once a month sharing water with the homeless. As time progressed, I would take them other things.

Not long afterward, I found out my daughter Dee was sick. We rushed her to the emergency room because her legs had swollen. The doctors said it was cellulitis and put her on medication. At the time, her husband was incarcerated and, once again, God brought her and the two children to live with me.

During Dee's illness, I had a dream about a father sitting in a room with his daughter who had cancer. I saw doctors putting the port in and the daughter having chemotherapy. It was so odd.

The medication wasn't working, so I took Dee back to the doctor a second time. This time, he did a cervical exam. So much blood poured from her that the doctor had to put a trash can under the table to catch the blood. He looked up, shook his head and said we needed a gynecologist as it looked like cervical cancer.

It was cancer, stage three. A month later it was stage four. She had chemo and radiation, but the cancer was so aggressive it had already metastasized throughout her body. I realized my dream was about us. I was the parent in the room with my daughter. God was preparing me.

I poured out my emotions to God during my early 4 a.m. writing time. I wrote about the pain, the struggle, the hurt, and all of my fear and questions. God would then give me scriptures and encouragement. He brought healing to my soul.

The words became poetry and I started writing a book, breathed by the Holy Spirit. Dee asked me to dedicate the book to her. I laughed, saying, "I have two daughters, not one." I did not know that within the year she would pass.

She spent her final three weeks at a hospice. As hard as it was for me to see her sick, it was harder to watch my grandchildren, ages ten and fifteen, care for their mother during her worst times. They were so brave.

Her kids and I, along with my oldest daughter Char, and several other family members, sang to Dee as she took her last breath. She was my baby girl. I cannot even begin to say what it was like to lose her, and to see my grandchildren suffer the loss of their mother.

I put my grief aside for them, knowing they would never have their mother to see their life achievements. The loss took me down a dark road. "God, I know You love me," I would say. "I prayed for healing. I believed You would heal her." My faith was strong, and I believed God could do anything.

Dee was so loving. She was the one to always plan parties and get the family together. She was vibrant and joyful. Watching her loose energy during those last months of her life was painful.

Yet she kept smiling. She died with so much grace. She even touched the lives of people in the hospice who cared for her. She had such a sweet spirit. She was comforting others while she was dying. Looking back, I see her death as a healing, not here on earth, but on the other side.

Dee's ten-year old son is the same as his mama. While visiting her at the hospice, he encouraged others and prayed with them. It was precious. He inspired me as I wrote during my early mornings. God prepared me for the days that still laid ahead. Dee gave me custody of her precious children, and I had to be strong to help them go through the grief process.

About a year later, I had another dream. This time of my daughter, Char. I dreamt she went into a room, and we were looking for her, but we couldn't find her. Shortly after that, Char wasn't feeling too well. She was already on meds for Lupus. Now and then, she'd have a bad spell where her joints ached, then she would feel better and go back to work. One Friday morning, I received a call telling me Char was going on her fourth day at home. She was having trouble breathing and couldn't walk, and was rushed to the ER.

I raced the four-hour trip to Atlanta and arrived at the hospital where I sat with her and prayed with her. She had a lot of pain breathing. I remember her saying her legs were dry, and she scratched them. I lovingly rubbed her legs down with lotion, and then the doctor came in.

They had run tests and he said Char had pneumonia and they needed to put her on a ventilator to help her breathe. The next morning, a Saturday, they took her for treatment and she never recovered. They tried to revive her three times, but she passed.

It was just like my dream where she went into a room and I couldn't find her. I realized I wouldn't find her, not on this earth. At that moment, it felt like I wouldn't find her—ever.

I was in shock. Her death happened so suddenly. She was such a champion when her sister passed. She spoke out about cervical cancer, encouraging women to have exams. I knew I was strong after Dee passed, but I could not handle this. I had no more children. I lost all three. My heart goes out to parents who lose their children. I don't try to understand how they feel; I know how they feel. I miss my girls so much. I will never be the same.

I will forever miss my every day phone calls from my girl. I will never hear her voice say, "I love you! Have a good day." It's indescribable. There are no words as to how losing her made me feel. One day she was there, and the next day she was gone.

How could this happen again? How am I supposed to go on? How can I watch three more grandchildren endure the loss of their mother? How can I be strong for them? I had so many questions. Watching the devastation on my grandchildren's faces was the worst part.

There were many days after that I didn't want to get up out of bed. I didn't want to see anybody or talk to anybody. The pain was, and can still be, so unbearable. I'd say to God, "I know you can raise the dead. Please raise them and take me. Let them be here for their children."

Still, He gives me the ability to place one foot in front of the other. It's as if He refuses to let me fall. He gives me His strength every day.

Now, I see why He woke me up every morning, giving me those scriptures. I have His Word in me so I can draw from it when I feel weak. His Word is where I find my strength. I'm so thankful I have an intimate relationship with God. Having God's Word so firmly ingrained in me that I can say it out loud when I have no strength, when there is no will in me, is the only way I've made it. When His words pour through my lips they are life-giving. His Word is powerful. It is outside of me.

God continued to develop His purpose for my life, which required deeper giving. My calling has expanded from bringing water to the homeless, to raising funds and providing a home for single homeless women. The ministry of giving help to the homeless has opened a place in my life to share with others who need hope and encouragement.

Sometimes, I receive calls from people who are suicidal. Each time, the Holy Spirit gives me the right words to say. I'm not just providing for the homeless, but I'm giving to the hopeless.

So many times, we can't hear God because we're too busy. We get swept up in our problems. Believe me, I was swept up in my troubles in my earlier years. We have to be still and rest in order to hear Him. Regardless of what we go through, we can make it through if God's Word is deeply embedded in us during times of stillness.

There is Divine Rest for our busy, troubled souls. It's real, I know.

To learn more about Georgette, contribute toward her work, or to purchase her book, 30 Days of Divine Rest: A Collection of heartfelt poems and lessons from my Heavenly Father, visit www.GeorgetteDJackson.com.

*We never know how high we are till we are called to rise;
and then, if we are true to plan, our statures touch the skies.*
Emily Dickinson

PART SIX

Together We Are Stronger

Because of Personality and Emotion

Together We Are Stronger
Because of Personality and Emotion

It is such a gift to understand one another's personality style and to read emotions. In reality, it is a necessity. What a difference it would make if we could learn these things at school. We gain knowledge and learn skills for careers, yet we do not have a clue how to work with one another. Whether in the workplace, community or home, it positively changes our behavior when we understand each other's strengths, weaknesses, responses to pressure, and love languages. Understanding why someone works, says and acts the way they do goes a long way in giving respect and love that endures life's challenges.

There are many personality tests and it's worth taking a few of them to dig into one's own self. The more we understand ourselves, the more we can understand others—we are all different, yet the same. One personality test I often use with my clients is the DISC Behavior Profile. All behavior is modifiable with work. Another fun assessment to complete focuses on the Five Love Languages. Knowing one another's love language can help us to appreciate when another person is loving us with their language. How easy it is for us to feel unloved, when we actually are loved, but don't feel loved because the other person is not speaking our love language.

Feelings are our unspoken thoughts—the body's expression of our thoughts. Emotions are powerful human communication tools that can harm, hurt, bring peace or joy to ourselves and others. It would serve each of us well to learn how to detect our own emotional responses to situations and people. How much healthier we would be to learn how to cope with and deescalate our feelings when needed, and how to access them if they're deeply hidden. Unacknowledged emotions bubble up from under the surface and can cause feelings of being overwhelmed, disconnected, anxious, and stressed. It becomes a problem when we unleash negative emotions randomly and inappropriately. It is worth getting the help needed to work through challenges and trauma from our past and daily stressors.

We are truly all so the same,
Not wanting to live a life of shame,
Yet so different.
Each one so magnificent.

It's a beautiful thing,
So throw your hat in the ring.
Let each one sing
Their different song.

Accepting space to belong,
Giving and receiving respect.
Creating the circle effect
To grow and love as we connect.

Emra Smith

We met at a Leader's Summit in Austin, Texas. It was a small intimate group and by the end of the weekend a bond had forged. During the year that followed, we became sisters. Our ethnicity, countries of origin, current homelands oceans apart, varied skin color, and accents don't matter. We laugh together, share the wonder, and at times fears, of the call on our lives to empower women globally. I continually learn from Tina what being bold for God means and to expect much from Him. There is nothing small about this woman who inspires me with her warmth and humor.

Tina Allton

The Power of One
Increasing the Power of Many

Ours was one of the wealthy families in Ghana, where money didn't equate to happiness. My father was an arrogant, rude man who disrespected others, including his five children. My mom, a successful business woman, filled our turbulent home by adopting many children. We had up to 11 kids in our home.

Always being small, I was constantly bullied, but I found solace in reading and learning. I would read about Koffi Anan, Oprah, and Tintin and I knew there was more to life, that I had to focus, get good grades and leave my homeland. I knew I could do it as my beautiful, intelligent grandma motivated, mentored and encouraged me to be the best person I could be. She made me feel so good about myself and challenged me to dig deep, no matter what happened around me.

Till this day, the lessons she taught me are deeply ingrained in me. She said to always figure out where my boundaries are, and that the world is bigger than you can see. It's like climbing to the top of a wall; you get bruised and hurt, but you keep going up. Circumstances don't determine what your future will be, you determine what you want and must work hard for it.

It seems as if I always lived an independent life. While at home, I hid in the shadows and left home for boarding school at age eight. My life changed at age 13 when I learned about Jesus, and that He was a loving dad. It was such a big relief to know that I was truly loved and that He was always interested in me. I could just sit and talk and He would listen. I still see God this way. I imagine He sits in the passenger seat as I drive. I may not see Him, but He's there, I just need to believe it. It was freeing to know that I had a different Father who was always there and so interested in me, one I didn't have to beg for anything. I latched onto really getting to know Him. So amazing!

As a young adult, I spent a year in national service. After that, I completed University and four days later I ran away from home. I couldn't cope with the negativity and constantly begging to have any slightest need met. I hated always feeling like a burden to my dad. I wanted to go to London. I told mom she could either help me or lose me. She knew I was a straight shooter and that I meant it. She bought me a flight and sent me off with a 100 pounds.

My first year in London, I served in the home I found residence in. I cleaned, cooked, and worked three jobs. Eventually, I received my University transcript, started teaching, and got my own place.

Then I met Peter and entered into one of the most difficult times of my life. I had never been in a relationship before and had no knowledge of men. I fell pregnant with twins and following complications, lost one of the babies.

I felt broken inside as I was rushed to hospital. I had let myself and God down by living outside of God's plan for my life, having lived with a man outside of marriage. I felt unworthy of God's love. My friend assured me that God was with me, still loved me, always has grace, and forgives.

I prayed, repented, and asked Him to let me feel something different. I asked Him to show Himself to me, to give me a physical manifestation of His presence in my life. I wanted to know He heard me, and that He would help me.

I learned about grace that day at the hospital. I went in for surgery and when they did the scan they saw that the remaining baby had grown. The doctors were stunned at such an impossibility they couldn't understand. God had given me a sign, He revealed to me that He heard me, that He was with me. Now, I had to move on from that place of pain. Yet I felt totally alone, isolated.

Some years later, Peter and I married. I remember thinking and hoping that everything would be alright now that we were in a marriage relationship. How wrong I was. The difficulties were intensified with the complexities of blending his other children into our family. The journey with their mother was not easy and painful years followed. Insecurity wrapped cold fingers around me and seeped into our relationship as time dragged by. My husband's ex tormented and oppressed me in a myriad of ways—arguing, insulting, even verbally abusing me in public. At times, I felt like a prisoner in my own life, free but trapped around every turn.

I fell pregnant and lapsed into fear of my daughter being rejected because she was my child. Once again, I was the outsider in the family and I felt so alone. After a complicated pregnancy, I had our daughter. My heart sank and I succumbed to the seeds planted in my mind, feeling she wasn't seen as special, loved, or wanted. I spiraled into postnatal depression. I couldn't feed my tiny little girl and struggled to bond with her. I pushed myself through, knowing she needed me. Thankfully, I was going to counseling and taking medication for depression.

Ten months later I was pregnant again. I went in for the scan and found out the child was a boy. Knowing I was having a son filled me with joy as I drove home. Sadly, that afternoon a call came telling us that my father-in-law had a stroke. The stress of what that meant instantly took away my happiness. Our lives changed as we adapted our home so that Peter's parents could come stay with us while his father recovered from the stroke. How thankful we were for his good recovery.

Amidst all this, before I knew it, Brian was born. I had a long road to recovery after the C-section birth, but had finally learned to ask for help. I loved this little boy so much.

When Brian was about 11 months old, I was on my way home and waiting to turn right when a car came toward us at full speed. All I could say was, "Jesus save me." I closed my eyes, waiting for the impact. When I opened my eyes, I was on the other side of the road with cars hooting their horns all around me. I was so shaken, but my little boy was still asleep in the back seat.

Shaking, still trying to figure out what was going on, I prayed on the phone with a friend. As I was recovering from the shock of the accident, I found myself angry. Old voices from the past clamored and I found myself asking God why He allowed all of this to happen.

A few weeks later, an ambulance rushed by our home and stopped in front of Peter's older girls' home down the road—where his ex lived. The girls' mom had passed out. Once she arrived at the hospital she was in a coma and on life support. It wasn't long before they switched off the machines. We had to tell the girls that their mom passed away. The turmoil of our broken relationships left the girls believing I was happy their mom died. My resentment for the complexities of our blended family deepened.

I pleaded with God to not let me own any guilt or pain and to release me from the black hole I was plunged into. How thankful I am that I learned to be honest with God.

I poured out my despair to Him. "Where are You God?" I asked in prayer. "If you truly love me, take this baggage of resentment, fear, and depression and replace it with Your love in my heart for our family."

I often had memories of the girls' mom, and heard her hateful words echoing in my head. I'd found myself livid if I even heard her name or seeing her favorite color, purple.

"God take this away; take away the memory," I pleaded.

After my prayers, one of her daughters brought me flowers which were purple. I was amazed that I had NO angry emotions—they were all gone. That's when I knew God heard me. He removed it all. The bitter battle in my head was gone! God is good!

As a way to acknowledge what God had done, I went out and bought a purple outfit. Wearing it became a reminder of my covenant with God; a reminder that He took the darkness from me. Now the color reminds me that God heals, that God's presence is with me, and that His hand is over my life. It reminds me of the surety that I will keep trusting in Him, that He is never unfaithful.

A year after God's deliverance and restoration in my life, we discovered that my youngest step-daughter was a Type 1 Diabetic. She got mixed up in the wrong crowd and we did all we could do selflessly with love, but it was never enough. She struggled with self-esteem and the complexities of her life.

Once again my faith was tested, loving through God's grace was hard. The enemy whispered that I could not love enough. During this time, God strengthened our marriage and our home and we lived with God as our head. Choosing God as our support, our leader. We learned to pray together and were bonded together. We created the three-stranded cord, where God has made us stronger.

When God called us to make a difference in the lives of others, our ministry—Undefeeted—was born. It's our global nonprofit that brings knowledge, awareness and action to people who have diabetes in order to help them avoid the complications that all too often lead to lower limb amputations. An amputation due to diabetes happens every 20 seconds. 85 percent of those amputations could have been avoided.

Once we launched the nonprofit in the US, I found myself onstage speaking to 750 people. This led to my being invited to speak alongside Jermaine Jackson. Invitations followed and mentoring in business development grew.

God placed a group of God-fearing women around me. I hadn't lost my faith, but I needed the support, confidence and love. I found His renewed promises to me, seeing the enemy's lies in my life story. I saw and know that God had designed a big plan for my life and that His plans haven't changed. Through it all, the Lord restored my relationship with my step-daughter and I welcomed her graciousness and love to me.

God's call on my life for global work continues to grow in the most unexpected ways through launching Nations Of Women, NOW. I have learned to walk in faith and obedience, even when I'm afraid to say what I feel He lays on my heart. And believe me, He lays things on my heart!

Tina is the CEO of Tina Allton Consultancy and NOW, Co-Director of Circle Podiatry in the UK, Co-Founder of Undefeeted.org. She speaks to global audiences, is a mum to four, wife to Peter and loved by many. You can learn more about the work that Tina does at www.TinaAllton.com and www.NationsOfWomen.com

*The power of one, if fearless and focused, is formidable,
but the power of many working together is better.*
Gloria Macapagal Arroyo

I learned about Dawn's work as we set off for the first Hope Walk from Savannah, Georgia to Sarasota, Florida. We had the privilege of visiting with the ladies living in one of Dawn's Radical Restoration homes. The stories of the women were heart-wrenching, soul-stirring and powerful. Dawn and the women she reaches for Jesus are proof that nothing is impossible for God. Nothing!

Dawn Knighton-Adkins

From Prostitute to Pastor

I was one of those kids that longed to fit in and never did. My heart of giving and loving others was fueled by my need to belong. I loved to give my clothes, my mom's jewelry—anything to help other girls feel pretty. I loved church, learning about Jesus, and being baptized. In fact, I was baptized many times. I wanted the spiritual fire my aunt and uncle's country preacher had. As I listened to him speak, I felt like I was in the presence of God.

My zeal, fervor and energy for life spilled over and fueled the passion I directed toward my first love when I was fourteen. As we grew older and inseparable we started getting into trouble. We'd skip school together, which eventually led to us drinking, smoking pot and taking speed. We spent the weekends using acid and quaaludes. Cocaine soon followed. We then discovered how to get free drugs; we sold them.

By seventeen, I was married and pregnant with my first child. What a beautiful little girl she was! I adored her, yet I destroyed our relationship through my late nights out, drug use, and selling. My marriage also failed, yet as soulmates we were still in love stayed connected. A year later, he was killed in a car accident that left me devastated. That's when my life really began to spin out of control.

I married my new drug-dealing boyfriend and barely slept as we managed the "needs" of our large clientele around the clock. While taking a short nap one night, we were awakened by the thud of our door being kicked in. There was screaming and then cops' pistols aimed at our faces. We were busted. I got five months, as I was already on probation and pregnant. I was cuffed, went to prison, and pictured on the news and in the papers. I was facing the possibility of federal prison. By the grace of God and a praying mother-in-law, our charges were dropped through a technicality on the search warrant. What a wake-up call!

Fourteen months later, we had another gorgeous baby. I was glad I had escaped giving birth to my beautiful baby boy in prison. Life had taken a turn for good. I was determined to only social drink now and then, and smoke an occasional joint, until the kids were a little older. Once again I was drawn to the wrong crowd. This time, it was through my child's baseball team. One of the other moms shared cocaine with me. Before I knew it, I was drinking like a fish, staying out late, losing weight, and acting completely out of control. DUI's, writing bad checks, car accidents, and incarcerations led to another divorce.

My life became a pattern of relationship, marriage, drugs, jail. Eventually, I checked into a rehab. I started working as a hairdresser, and made good money. I tried mending my relationships with my children, AGAIN and again. I determined to use the tools I learned at rehab, and decided to moved with my ex-husband and start a new life in Florida. We registered him for college, found an apartment, enrolled the kids in school, and I worked cutting hair. Needing more money, I decided to work at a local bar. Really, I should have known better!

I wanted to give my kids a chance at life, so they went to stay with their grandparents as my life spiraled out of control AGAIN. Life grew worse as I ran around with sugar daddies, danced at strip clubs, worked for escort companies, and started sleeping with men I didn't know so I could get money for my next hit. The drugs helped numb my guilt and the horror of my choices. I made thousands of dollars, which I spent as soon as I got it. Money, men, materialism, and drugs ran my life. I'd marry men who'd pay my bills and manipulate everyone I came in contact with. I didn't value a living soul, especially myself.

Life moved along in a fog. I was so high I didn't remember my children's birthdays, or know the date, or time of day. My parents didn't know if I was dead or alive. I hated myself and couldn't bear to be sober. I never dreamed I could become like this. As my life spiraled down, so did the quality of men around me. I started robbing people. Abuse became the norm. I looked awful and my life was a nightmare. I even started seeing demons everywhere.

Then one day in late October 2003 at Biketoberfest in Daytona Beach, Florida, things became even worse. A man I was with turned against me. Instinctively, I knew I was in real trouble. Then he pulled out duct tape.

He immobilized me, taping my hands behind my back, and putting tape over my mouth. He started hitting my forehead with his pistol, spouting out all the horrific things he had done to tramps like me. "You all deserve to die," he said. He straddled me and started punching me. He busted my ribs, then knocked my teeth out. Blood started gushing from my mouth.

I cried out to God, "Please don't let me die like this." Instantly an overwhelming peace washed over me. I was watching his every move. As I prayed, I saw the man's face change. He started to gag and threw up all over me. Tears rolled down his face. Sobbing, he begged me to forgive him as he put his clothes on and fled. God literally saved my life.

I passed out and woke up in the hospital's rape crisis center. The nurse told me that I was not alone, yet I had never felt more alone in my life. I felt hopeless. I wish I had died. I was barely able to move. I asked myself, "Now what?"

I left the hospital hopeless and enraged, and soon found a gun and some dope. Things got really ugly. I'd promise men things, would blindfold them, then rob them. My addiction was out of control. I was smoking crack, shooting meth, and taking pills. I was on a suicide mission. I went from one derelict house to the next, getting robbed, shot at, stabbed, raped—used and abused. I spent my nights alternating between the street corner and jail. In jail, I raised all kinds of hell until the police would tie me to the black chair, or taser me to force me into confinement. They hated it when I was brought in.

I had a brief interlude of normalcy after finding Jesus in jail again, but Satan promptly sent two unassuming crackheads my way and it all began AGAIN—just worse. I was eating out of dumpsters and sleeping under bridges. I had burned every bridge and hurt each person that loved me or tried to help me. But God stayed. He protected me and heard my quiet cry.

One day, I was trying again to get clean and sober. I felt God call me to go to a house called Heaven's Gardens. It was a home for prostitutes and women like me. There I met Pastor Aida, who encouraged me and showed me the love of God. She took me to a conference in Orlando where the speaker, a woman who had been delivered from a life of prostitution, came down and prayed with me. Even though my life cycle of drugs continued, that spiritual experience stayed with me.

High on crack and meth one morning, I felt the presence of the Lord surround me, urging me to go church. I cleaned up at the shelter, and went to Pastor Aida's church. When the altar call came I ran forward and cried out to God. Pastor Dawn Raley came and laid hands on me. Even though I was back on the streets after that, I knew I had experienced an encounter with God. Two weeks later, I was busted and went to jail kicking and screaming. I was led straight to confinement, butt naked, and put in a straight jacket.

Here, in maximum security, I cried out to God. "Is there any way You can help me?" This time, He truly spoke to me and I heard. "You are valuable to Me, a precious jewel. I have put you in a safety deposit box." He was with me. He would heal me. He took me to a place of full surrender.

When they moved me to a single cell, I asked for a Bible. I wanted to know God, who He was. The more time I spent seeking His presence, the more I was able to see Jesus. Our intimacy grew and I could picture myself in His lap, leaning on His shoulder, crying through the pain. I saw myself snuggled up to Him, heard His heartbeat, and fell asleep in His arms.

Jesus showed me the prisons inside myself that I needed to breakout of, so that I could be healed and forgiven. Daily, we walked through each experience of my life, every person I hurt, and those that hurt me. I forgave and He forgave. Next, I had to forgive me.

Jesus assured me that He shed His blood so that I could be forgiven. He told me I must claim forgiveness. I fully surrendered my all to Him. I knew He loved me and died for me. The air was so thick with His presence, I felt hot from my head to my toes.

As I was reading Isaiah 61, I asked the Lord, "What could You possibly anoint me for? What could you ever use me to do?" He gave me a glimpse of my life and the many women that were the same as me. He gave me a clear, strong vision of having a house for women like myself. It seemed impossible.

I faced a fifteen-year prison term, but by God's grace was sentenced to six months in a Jail Addiction Treatment Program, plus a year and a day in prison. One night at the program God confirmed His call to me through Luke 4:18, the same words from Isaiah 61. God's transformation in my life began.

I started Bible studies and my cell became a prayer closet for the women. This season in prison became one of the best times of my life. God sent women to teach, pray over, and minister to me. I became so hungry for the Word that I signed up for Bible College. I wanted to retrain my brain and be transformed by Him.

One day, the Lord used me to pray over an inmate. For the first time, I saw someone released from a twenty-six year addiction from crack. As I fearfully prayed, I felt personal release. I was able to let go of the medications I was on for my diagnosis as bipolar and schizophrenic! I was euphoric. I promised God, "If You get me through this and deliver me for good, I will come back to this prison and tell everyone how real You are."

In the weeks and months that followed, I devoured the Word of God and saw Him in everything. He revealed my call—my life's work: I knew I was to go back to the streets and into the prisons to teach and preach His Word. I knew my life's journey had not been in vain. He gave me a vision to have houses where my sisters who found Jesus could go to when leaving prison.

God's grace filled my soul. Walking in His power, I entered life a new woman. I worked hard, went back to school at 41 years old, tithed, and spent the rest of my time counseling and encouraging others in the various places God led me to.

He taught me that the process I was going through was one of "Radical Restoration." I realized that would be the name of the ministry I would serve in—a ministry of discipleship, growth, development, and—ultimately—transformation.

Nine months after my release from prison, I shared my vision for a home for women. Miraculously, God provided a rental, money for the down payment, money to fix it up, money for electricity, and the first four women!

I continued to work hard at two jobs to raise the funds to keep the house going. I studied between work and started speaking and teaching in the prisons in Florida. God gave me a passion for helping others like myself to retrain our brains to a new way of thinking. We were removing false identities that the world or our past failures had given us, and restoring our true identities that God's Word gives us.

I remarried for the eighth time, committed to Jesus, and success in marriage. This time, through no wrong-doing of my own, it ended. That is a story for another day. You can also read it in my book.

There are so many stories of God's provision and expansion of the work He was doing in the first house, the next house, then the next, and the next . . . each house has a story of blind faith. I have learned that when God tells you to do something, it doesn't matter what people think. In John 2:5, Mary tells the disciples, "Whatever He tells you to do, DO IT." I knew I had to be obedient, even when He sent me back to Daytona Beach—another miracle story.

Eight years from the day I gave my life to Christ, I walked across a platform to receive my Doctorate in Theology and Biblical Counseling. There I was, the little girl who did poorly at school and had lived an unhealthy life in every manner possible as an adult. I absolutely knew that nothing was impossible with God.

The ministry God gave me has grown. We have built many houses, expanding the work from Florida to the Texas Offender Reentry Initiative (TORI), Alabama, and Indiana. When we surrender whole-heartedly to God, there is nothing that He won't do!"

To connect with Pastor Dawn, invite her to speak, consult, train, or lead a seminar on residential rehabilitation programs. To reach her, or for information about placement, email RadicalRestorationMinistries@gmail.com. To learn more about her ministry go to www.radicalrestorationministries.com.

Pastor Dawn's book, Radical Restoration, The Dawn Knighton Story, can be purchased on Amazon.

Everyone has inside of him a piece of good news.
The good news is that you don't know how great you can be!
How much you can love! What you can accomplish!
And what your potential is!
Anne Frank

CONCLUSION

Together We Are Stronger

In Conclusion

Speaking Up

> *The simple act of naming a bias as such or objecting to it on the spot, establishes a social atmosphere that discourages it: Saying nothing serves to condone it.*
> — Daniel Goleman

When you see disrespect, observe bias, prejudice, and exclusion at home, in the workplace, business, church or community, can you speak up and be part of making the situation better?

It is not always easy to speak up when we see others act differently from how we feel things should be. When I observe what I feel is a wrong, before I speak up, I ask myself if I am seeing the situation from my bias or from truth. I believe the approach we should take in any situation always centers on respect for others. Here are a few ways to help positively change a situation, and some questions to ask the people involved.

Assume good intent, but explain the impact of other's behaviors. "I know you mean well, but it hurts when . . ."

Ask questions to clarify. Not all responses given under pressure are a true reflection of the heart of a person. "What did you mean when you said . . . ?"

Interrupt and redirect the conversation when the timing and circumstances aren't right. "Let's not go there right now. Let's save that for another time."

Broaden the perspective to universal human behavior. "I think that applies to everyone . . ."

Determine if they are speaking of something personal. "Are you speaking of someone or something in particular?"

Take responsibility for your statements, never blame or point fingers. "I feel . . . It seems to me . . ."

As Gandhi said, "You must be the change you wish to see in the world." Don't condemn others or act out against them. Check your heart. Are you willing to be the one to take the time to understand, respect, and make room in your life for those that are different than you?

Take time to listen and learn about people who are not like you. Give yourself time to discover why it may be difficult to accept them and respect their point of view. Do the work needed to heal from hurt. Release control of needing to be right. These are the first steps. Following these steps is where the miracle of learning to LOVE begins.

Love others. Love ALL people. All people are miracles created by God. Being able to love people who are different from ourselves is evidence of the work God is doing in and through our lives.

My Prayer

Dear ones,
Let us not love
merely in theory,
With word or with tongue
giving lip service to compassion,
But in action and in truth
In practice and in sincerity,
Because practical acts of love
Are more than words.

1 John 3:18

With thanks

Thank you to each of the ladies who shared your stories. It takes courage to share. Your stories inspire me each time I read them, and I know they will touch many other lives as well.

By sharing, you show how everything is possible with God, even when it seems impossible. You prove God truly changes the hearts of humans, enabling us to live in respect of one another with love.

Each one of you is a woman of impact because you live the change you wish to see in the world. Thank you for saying yes to including your story in this book, for knowing that Together we are Stronger.

Thank you Lisa Luckett and Carol Ogle for taking the time to review and edit this book filled with stories of hope and teaching. I value your time, love and energy.

Thank you Rachael Hartman for always being in my author corner. You are an anchor I trust with my publishing. I so appreciate you!

Abundant, humble, thanks to God. Some moments I can dance and sing and shout my love, thanks, and adoration from the rooftops, marveling at who He is and how He works in us. Other times I'm hushed, face covered, kneeling in respect and awe, with no words, just my heart.

All I can say is thank You for using me, and creating in me a voice for those that are different, yet the same. Thank You for the years you worked on me that have culminated in this book.

Thank You. You do make all things work together for good. Together, with You, we are stronger.

#TogetherWeAreStronger

About the Author

Emra Smith

Emra Smith is an inspirational challenger and facilitator of HOPE. Her passion for teaching diversity and inclusion, was birthed from her life story as an "outsider." She was a white Afrikaans girl who grew up in an English community in South Africa. Her childhood was a time where there was no freedom of press, which kept apartheid invisible to her. As an adult, after moving from South Africa to the USA, she learned of the atrocities that had occurred in her country, and of those that continue to happen throughout the world.

The many little stories within her big story, shaped her, compelled her, to a career of speaking and corporate training. As a life coach, her heart for understanding the challenges of women intensified and set her on a path to gather and share stories that teach and inspire. She loves to help women find purpose in the chaos of life, motivating and teaching them how to truly love one another.

Emra is a Certified Coach through Coach Training Alliance. She has successfully completed Licensure and Specialty-Certification as a New Life Story® Wellness Coach. Her expertise in the psychology and neuroscience of coaching extends her considerable experience in Life Coaching.

Emra started speaking and teaching as a teenager in her church, and continued to speak throughout her Marketing and Sales career.

She became a Corporate Trainer in the Hospitality Industry and further specialized in Diversity and Inclusion, and Effective Communication. Emra speaks to various organizations and churches and has won numerous awards and contests at Toastmasters.

Emra has differentiated herself through her unique and powerful inspirational speaking which she pours into each topic and training.

She is the Founder and CEO of the International School of Story, a place and platform where women give and receive HOPE. She helps empower women to boldly step into their stories. She teaches skills to cope with stress, anxiety and depression, and to live victoriously despite life's traumas.

To invite Emra to speak, host a workshop or training, or to begin coaching with her, visit www.emrasmith.com or email her at emra@emrasmith.com.

For more about The International School of Story and to be a part of the global platform where women share HOPE through stories, visit www.internationalschoolofstory.org.

A division of International School of Story
Savannah, Georgia

www.marigoldpressbooks.org

www.ingramcontent.com/pod-product-compliance
Lightning Source LLC
Chambersburg PA
CBHW050324120526
44592CB00014B/2036